Youth Ask

A

MODERN
PROPHET

about Life, Love, and God

Also by Harold Klemp

The Art of Spiritual Dreaming
Ask the Master, Books 1 and 2
Autobiography of a Modern Prophet
Child in the Wilderness
A Cosmic Sea of Words: The ECKANKAR Lexicon
The Language of Soul
The Living Word, Books 1 and 2
Love—The Keystone of Life
A Modern Prophet Answers Your Key Questions about Life
Past Lives, Dreams, and Soul Travel
Soul Travelers of the Far Country
The Spiritual Exercises of ECK
The Spiritual Laws of Life
The Temple of ECK
The Wind of Change
Your Road Map to the ECK Teachings: ECKANKAR Study Guide

The Mahanta Transcripts Series
Journey of Soul, Book 1
How to Find God, Book 2
The Secret Teachings, Book 3
The Golden Heart, Book 4
Cloak of Consciousness, Book 5
Unlocking the Puzzle Box, Book 6
The Eternal Dreamer, Book 7
The Dream Master, Book 8
We Come as Eagles, Book 9
The Drumbeat of Time, Book 10
What Is Spiritual Freedom? Book 11
How the Inner Master Works, Book 12
The Slow Burning Love of God, Book 13
The Secret of Love, Book 14
Our Spiritual Wake-Up Calls, Book 15
How to Survive Spiritually in Our Times, Book 16

Stories to Help You See God in Your Life
The Book of ECK Parables, Volume 1
The Book of ECK Parables, Volume 2
The Book of ECK Parables, Volume 3
Stories to Help You See God in Your Life, ECK Parables, Book 4

MAHANTA

This book has been authored by and published under the supervision of the Mahanta, the Living ECK Master, Sri Harold Klemp. It is the Word of ECK.

Youth Ask
A
MODERN
PROPHET
about Life, Love, and God

_____

HAROLD KLEMP

ECKANKAR
Minneapolis

Youth Ask a Modern Prophet about Life, Love, and God

Copyright © 2004 ECKANKAR

Printed in U.S.A.
Compiled by Dawn McKenna Miller and the ECK youth
Edited by Joan Klemp, Anthony Moore, and Mary Carroll Moore
Text illustrations by Stan Burgess
Cover photos by Montina Holliday and Robert Huntley

Publisher's Cataloging-in-Publication

(Provided by Quality Books, Inc.)

Klemp, Harold.
    Youth ask a modern prophet about life, love, and God / Harold Klemp.
        p. cm.
        SUMMARY: Harold Klemp, spiritual leader of Eckankar, answers questions pertaining to subjects like morality and patriotism posed by young people.
        Audience: Ages 13–25.
        LCCN 2004107222
        ISBN 1-57043-203-1

    1. Eckankar (Organization)—Doctrines—Juvenile literature. 2. Klemp, Harold—Views on life—Juvenile literature. 3. Spiritual life—Eckankar (Organization) —Juvenile literature. 4. Love—Juvenile literature. 5. God—Juvenile literature. [1. Eckankar (Organization) —Doctrines. 2. Klemp, Harold—Views on life. 3. Spiritual life—Eckankar (Organization) 9. Love. 10. God. I. Title.

BP605.E3Y68 2004   299'.93
                                        QBI33-2057

CONTENTS

God? • What Are Co-workers with God? • One Can Become an ECK Master • Remembering Better • Aspects of the Mahanta • Personal Dialogues • What Is a Spiritual Name? • Did You Grow Up an ECKist? • ECK Masters Have Friends • What Does the Living ECK Master Aspire To? • The ECK Is My Heartbeat • ECK Masters Work in Harmony with the Mahanta • Peddar Zaskq • ECK Masters among the Native Americans • Simha • Kata Daki • Towart Managi • Continuous Line of Adepts • Want to Meet an ECK Master? • Love and Love Alone • *Workbook: Who Are The ECK Masters?*

INTRODUCTION

Lots of pundits have waxed eloquent about the young. Some of the insights are remarkable for their wisdom.

A Chinese proverb notes: "A young branch takes on all the bends that one gives it." A Scottish proverb says it's "Better [to] eat brown bread in your youth than in your age." May I add my two bits? "Enjoy youth; it lasts but a while."

For all that, youth is a tempestuous age. It's a time of storms and uncertainty in the midst of sunshine and laughter. But savor its taste anyway.

Questions do crop up for the young, however. They rise by the dozen, by the score—like weeds.

"What should I do when . . . ?"

Go it alone? Trust to street smarts? Fake it? Yes, those are possibilities, but so often they turn down a rocky, thorny road—a road of endless sorrow, grief, and pain. Sometimes it pays to lend an ear to one who's been over the route and bears the cuts and bruises of many mistakes.

Is today's youth, the future of tomorrow, going to hell in a basket? Not from my vantage point as a

Enjoy youth; it lasts but a while.

1

Youth wonder about things of God, of Spirit, of love.

spectator of the game. Overall, the youth are doing fine.

To see how well, take a quick look to appreciate the kinds of questions youth often ask about just getting along. School. Dating. Classmates' teasing. The loss of a loved one—pet or human. How did life start? AIDS? Picking a career. Karma. Choosing a mate for life.

The questions range so far and wide. Big horizons. Bigger visions.

Above all, these questions reveal a deep concern about more weighty matters than simply diversity and a host of other social and political issues.

Youth wonder about things of God, of Spirit, of love.

The youth in Eckankar are no lightweights. They're Souls come back to earth. In fact, they've been here many lifetimes in the past, sometimes even longer than their elders. But birth has scrubbed all past-life memories clean. So they've forgotten the particulars of old lessons of long ago. Still, they persist. Isn't there order behind the seeming madness of living?

What an honor to pass along to them my ideas on things. It's always a pleasure to share the Eckankar view. Yet what they choose to do with it is their own affair.

This collection of questions and answers stands on steady feet.

These questions from youth will astonish you with the depth and breadth of their concerns. Pull up a chair. Join us as we deal with the real, down-to-earth quandaries of living today.

Who knows? You may even catch a glimpse of yourself.

The spiritual student taps into the Supreme Creative Force to guide him around the blocks in his path.

1

How to Live and Make It in This World

The Spiritual Purpose of Problems

Can you explain why we have problems?

Troubles that come to us are for our purification. They come to us because we must learn a divine law.

Divine Spirit will use the most negative situation to teach us, and we wonder, *Why has God forsaken me?* God has not forsaken us. We are unwilling to give up certain passions of the mind and take the next step in our spiritual development. Habits fall away once Soul (you) decides It really wants spiritual realization more than Its vices.

The spiritual life is not meant to finally end the succession of problems, for they are given as opportunities for Soul's unfoldment. What the spiritual student does develop, however, is the inner link with the

Troubles that come to us are for our purification. They come to us because we must learn a divine law.

> Soul, the spiritual being you are, gains experience as It works through these rough spots on the road.

Ways I can handle conflicts with a loving heart:

ECK, the Holy Spirit. Thus he taps into the Supreme Creative Force that guides him around all the blocks in his path that once defeated him.

One's ability to take charge of his own life increases. This is a solid step toward self-mastery and that state of consciousness called the kingdom of heaven.

Learning about the Loving Heart

Why don't troubles go away once we ask for help?

Much of the trouble we have in life is a result of some long-standing negative attitude. It has created these situations. Soul, the spiritual being you are, gains experience as It works through these rough spots on the road.

Some of our troubles will be dispelled by Divine Spirit while others are not. They are part of the divine plan for Soul to gain the purification or change in consciousness so It can know what It is. It needs to know why It has reincarnated into today's family and business environment.

Many people do not understand that life, with its burdens, is a treasure. The weight of disappointment makes us close our eyes to the gift of being in the world to learn about the loving heart.

Handling Conflicts from a Higher Viewpoint

A friend is always trying to draw me into her conflicts. How do I handle this problem, since she is very close to me?

There are people who try to draw others into their problems. Their own troubles are overwhelming because they like the attention from others.

Of course, how much you choose to become a part of her world is for you to decide. But don't feel guilty if you want to pull out of the situation because it interferes with your life.

She has to make up her own mind about personal decisions. If her inner guidance gives her a direction, fine. All her decisions have to be her own.

You may act as a listening post if you want to. But don't let her take your life away from you.

What Mistakes Mean

I have always been afraid of making mistakes. I can't seem to let go of this attitude. Can you help?

Learning means making errors. Those who are learning spiritually make errors just the way anyone does when he is growing.

I don't mind an error as long as the individual benefits from it, picks up the pieces, and goes on—a wiser individual.

Tips on Self-Discipline

Can you help me with my self-discipline?

Each one of us in the lower worlds of time, space, and matter is struggling with self-discipline. We find it in everything we do, in our job or at home. It means, Can I get up in the morning on time? We have all these little things in our lives which are teaching us greater discipline.

I can't give you self-discipline, motivation, or even spirituality. In fact I can't give you anything. All I can do is help you in your own efforts. First of all, you have to figure out what your goal is.

Your goal can be anything, but it should be God-Realization. Not in the limited sense we've understood in orthodox religions, but in the sense of becoming one with Divine Spirit. Once we set that as our goal, then it depends on how fervently we want it.

> Learning means making errors. Those who are learning spiritually make errors just the way anyone does when he is growing.

What self-discipline means to me now:

The true reason for spiritual enlightenment is not to escape this life but to learn how to live it richly, to enjoy it.

How I can be happier:

Every so often you'll see a high-school student going down the street with a basketball in hand. Everywhere he goes he's got his basketball. He dribbles here, he dribbles there. It looks like the guy's lost his mind, but it's that kind of devotion that's needed to get a goal. He wants to be the best player.

What are you really looking for? What are you expecting the ECK, the Holy Spirit, to do for you, and how do you expect to be different?

Often we want enlightenment because the life we have today is hard. We have pains, aging starts catching up with us, the body won't run like it used to. But the true reason for spiritual enlightenment is not to escape this life but to learn how to live it richly, to enjoy it.

It's up to us to put the effort into it, to develop the self-discipline to practice the spiritual exercises of ECK.

Being Happier

How can we be happy when we have difficult experiences in our life?

Usually we're not happy then. The difficulty takes up all our time and attention. But it's later, when an old relationship, for example, is replaced by a new and better one, that the sunbeam of happiness again finds us.

Life is a stream of happy and unhappy experiences, because that leads to Soul's purification.

How do you get by in the dark times? Try to give love to someone, especially then.

Check Your Values

How can I balance my busy college life with my spiritual studies? How can I keep from becoming a spiritual derelict?

Don't worry, you won't become a spiritual derelict as long as you love God.

Nearly everyone shares the problem of having too little time for important things. It's hard to keep up. There are so many duties, like those of family, school, and business—let alone those of your spiritual studies.

The beauty of the Eckankar teachings is that you can fit them to your style of living. But keep one thing in mind. How much worth does any activity have without the influence of ECK (Holy Spirit) upon you? Check your values.

The Spiritual Exercises of ECK are the way to keep in touch with the Mahanta, the Inner Master. He is an expression of the Spirit of God that is always with you.

So don't risk the loss of your inner guidance. Make a list. Of all the important things you need to do each day, put the spiritual exercises right at the top.

They'll help you understand the nonsense in this world.

> Of all the important things you need to do each day, put the spiritual exercises right at the top.

What is important to me? What are my values?

Always Do Your Best

I have a teacher who does not have the best interest of her students at heart. It is difficult to learn in this type of environment. What can I do in this situation?

Some of my best teachers were monsters—or at least I thought so at the time.

Whether in school or in the workplace, we'll always run into people whose values appear to be much less than could be desired. A teacher, of course, has a duty to teach a subject. But here the human element comes in. Some teachers cannot teach, just as some students cannot learn.

Ask your classmates a question in private: Apart from this teacher, who was the worst teacher they

> A hard teacher can teach the virtue of work. An unfair teacher can remind you to develop fairness with others.

Teachers I've had and what I've learned from them:

ever had? Remember to also ask them about their best teacher.

A dull teacher can teach you patience. A hard teacher can teach the virtue of work. An unfair teacher can remind you to develop fairness with others. An incompetent teacher can teach you compassion. An insensitive teacher can teach you diplomacy and grace.

No matter what, always do your best.

When Classmates Tease

My sister is always being teased in school. Whenever she tells me and my mother about it, I get an inner nudge to say something to help her feel better. But I can never think of anything to say. Do you know of something I can say or do?

There are two reasons people tease each other: they either like someone or they don't. A boy may tease a girl because he likes her. It's a way he gets her to notice him. If this is what's happening to your sister, just say, "Aw, it's because he likes you."

A girl may also cause others to tease her. What's your sister doing to get teased?

Sometimes classmates tease somebody who gets angry over nothing. They try to get an angry person mad. All you can tell her then is this, "Stop getting mad and they won't have anything to tease you about."

Sometimes a child is teased because others are jealous of him or her. This often happens to a child who is very smart or pretty. Then the best thing to do is to smile and try to make a light joke of it. But don't get angry. That just makes it worse.

Tell your sister, "Think of Wah Z (my spiritual name), the Inner Master. He is always with you. Think of his love for you. Then their teasing can't hurt you."

Facing Ourselves

 *What should I do when people pick on me physically, emotionally, mentally, or verbally? This problem seems to have a strong hold on my life.*

Life, through other people and situations, faces us with ourselves.

It makes the weak stronger. The shy learn to be more outgoing. Helpless people are thrown upon their own resources, forcing them to help themselves. A popular song some years ago said, "Freedom's just another word for nothing left to lose." It was talking about an inner frame of mind.

Be strong to the strong. Show kindness to the weak. Use resourcefulness to deal with people and situations that cause you problems. Life brings us face-to-face with ourselves.

In your case, keep your attention firmly fixed upon the Mahanta. Sing HU, a love song to God, inwardly at the first sign of trouble. (HU is pronounced like the word *hue* and sung in a long, drawn-out note.)

You need to gain the wisdom to learn when to show strength, give a helping hand, or use your head to steer clear of danger. Once we've cast our lot to go a certain direction in life, it takes a steady determination to turn back a negative momentum and live for a good purpose in the future.

If it's any consolation, every Soul must eventually face every test. The only salvation lies in keeping HU upon our lips.

Overcoming Negative Attitudes

How can I feel the love of God while surrounded by people with negative attitudes? It seems so difficult.

> Life, through other people and situations, faces us with ourselves.

> What are the people and situations in my life teaching me about myself?

It is difficult. There are two things you can do: (1) Be polite when these people are near you, but sing HU, the love song to God, silently. Listen to them while you sing HU, rather than getting into a long conversation with them. Say as little as possible while still remaining cordial. (2) In your imagination, see the Mahanta near you.

The negative power is using them as its channels to see whether you will agree with their opinions. And by the way, the Mahanta is also watching your response to the negative power. Each confrontation is a test.

Habits

I would like to know why people develop habits. For example, I bite my nails.

Sometimes people start to bite their fingernails because of nervousness. Once it becomes a habit, they just keep on. For them, a fingernail is like a cigarette is to a smoker: a friend who is always there. How do you stop biting your fingernails? Bite your toenails instead. (I'm just teasing.)

Cravings

I'm having trouble with eating junk food. I eat it because I have cravings. Then I feel bad and get sick. What can I do to help myself stop?

Cravings often develop into destructive habits, as in your case. There's no easy way to break a bad habit.

But first try to find the reasons for your cravings. Is your body getting enough good nutrition? Chances are it isn't, if you're filling up on junk food. Maybe your parents can help find a dietitian to develop a good diet for you. But let's be honest, that's probably not going to work. Habits are very hard to break.

There's no easy way to break a bad habit.

But first try to find the reasons for your cravings. Is your body getting enough good nutrition?

Habits I need help with:

Imagine giving them to Divine Spirit.

Sometimes we eat because we feel we're not getting enough love. This stage can occur a lot of times in life. For example, now you're growing up. You're leaving the age of a young child, who gets most things done for it by parents, and are moving into a time of life where they (and everyone else) expect you to care more for yourself. Parents dress and undress babies and young children, and put away their clothes, and keep their room in order. As you get older now, do those things for yourself.

That last sentence gets to the heart of overeating due to feelings of not getting enough love. To get love, you must first give love—as an *older* child. A way to give love is by doing things for yourself. That's loving yourself.

So, to get love, you must first give love. For others to love you, you must be lovable. Start by loving yourself. How? You begin to put away your clothes and keep your room in order.

Here's the reason it's so important to love yourself in the first place: Others will only love you if you learn to love yourself first. To get love, give love. Love yourself first and other people will too.

There are about ten more things to say about getting over bad habits, but I'll tell them to you in your dreams. Pay attention.

Treat Yourself Gently

Over the past couple of years, I have developed a receding hairline. Is there a spiritual lesson to my hair loss? Am I working off karma or is there an imbalance in my life?

Losing hair can teach us to have respect for what many people take for granted.

Hair loss has dogged me ever since I was your age. It finally dawned on me that I had chosen a family

> To get love, you must first give love. For others to love you, you must be lovable. Start by loving yourself.

Things I can do to love myself more:

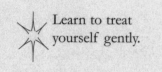

Learn to treat yourself gently.

Some problems that have made me stronger are:

where this was a problem for about half the males. A genetic weakness. But I learned to do something about it.

I learned to cut back on fatty foods. It also worked to use a shampoo that cleaned away sebum from the scalp. And to towel dry my hair gently. Nutrition plays a big role, of course.

But a full head of hair is only a superficial adornment. Many fine people are bald. Baldness is a part of their attraction.

Solve the baldness problem, and down the road comes the greying problem. Learn to treat yourself gently. It really is more important what's inside you than on your head.

Problems Make Us Strong

I'm eleven years old, and my grandma died recently. That night, right before I went to bed, she came to my room as Soul. She called my name and said, "I love you. I will miss you. I am waiting for some more people to say good-bye to, and then I'm needed elsewhere." I miss her and I'm really sad.

I'm also having a problem at school. I feel like I have no friends. My best friend betrayed me, and only one classmate will play with me at recess. I'm feeling so blue. What can I do?

Thank you for your thoughtful letter. Many of the problems of loss, betrayal, and some doubt about your self-worth have become less. The ECK (Holy Spirit) continues to guide your affairs in the direction that will help you most in a spiritual sense. Keep faith in the Mahanta, your inner guide.

Problems of one sort or another are always with us in some form or other. They are to make us strong. (Sometimes, though, we feel we're strong enough for now.)

Betrayal teaches us the pain of such an act. The lesson: not to betray another.

Loss can wound us deeply, but it will be with us from birth to translation (death). Lesson: to gain all the strength from it we can—then leave it behind and move on.

Was It Courage?

Almost every day people come up to me and speak negatively of someone, or I hear people around me gossiping. I have noticed that even when I do not support what they are saying, they lower my opinion about that individual.

What can I do to avoid getting involved in this gossip?

Once when I was a freshman in high school, four of my roommates were gossiping about our other roommate. Their comments were sharp, biting, and largely untrue. I was only half listening to them but noticed, as you have, that their opinions were having a bad effect on me.

Suddenly, these words dropped from my lips: "Won't anybody here speak up for Bill?"

All four turned to glare at me. It was very uncomfortable, because I had not meant to embarrass anyone, especially since two of them were sophomores. But my question broke up the group. After that, they chose their words more carefully around me.

Was it courage that had made me speak up for Bill? In a way, yes. The Mahanta had given me the words to speak, but I had to speak them. The Inner Master was

> Problems of one sort or another are always with us in some form or other. They are to make us strong.

Use this space for your own journal:

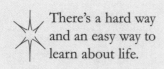 There's a hard way and an easy way to learn about life.

What this means to me:

already guiding me then, years before I first heard of Eckankar.

What I did may not work in your case. But listen to the Inner Master the next time such an occasion arises, and you will know what to do or say.

Is It True, Is It Necessary, Is It Kind?

Who do you listen to if your inner guidance tells you that something is all right for you to do, but your parent or someone else deserving of respect tells you that you may not?

That depends upon what our so-called inner guidance tells us to do. Instead of coming from the Mahanta, the guidance may be from the negative power, which is called the Kal in Eckankar. The whole purpose of the teachings of ECK is to teach us the difference.

Growing up, spiritually and physically, means that more and more people are affected by what we do. When a four-year-old boy hits his younger brother on the head with his hand, his parents see no great harm is done, because the child has so little strength. Therefore, the child gets a mild rebuke.

But let's say the child grows up. Now he's fifteen. He strikes a classmate in a fit of anger and hurts him. Will his punishment be as light as when he was a child? Again, it depends upon what provoked his anger—belligerence or self-defense.

Most people make impulsive decisions while under the control of the passions of the mind. This has nothing to do with the inner guidance of the Mahanta. They are selfish human beings who think only of their own gratification. In this case, they must suffer the consequences of their runaway emotions.

There's a hard way and an easy way to learn about life. If you've ever tried a new game in the video arcade, you can lose a handful of quarters in no time while trying to learn the game by yourself. A better way is to watch someone who has played the game before and imitate him.

Parents and teachers are role models for us. They do not have all the answers, but they are responsible for their children's entry into society as mature individuals. If they cannot do the job, then the Kal sees to it that the courts limit the destructive behavior of their children.

The older you become, the more you find there is no right or wrong in an absolute sense. The guiding rule that will stand you well throughout life is this ECK saying: Is it true, is it necessary, is it kind?

Unless the answer is yes for all three, then you would do well to reconsider your intended action.

That saying will resolve many of the problems that are facing you now in trying to understand the conflict you feel between your inner guidance and the guidance of your parents and others.

Finding Peace

What happens when two people get inner guidance in different directions? How can they resolve this, and why did it happen anyway?

There are two answers to this riddle. First, one or the other did not hear the Mahanta correctly. That is usually the case. Second, they both got the Master's message wrong.

The possible remedy is to have a neutral third party help sort out the pieces. Ask to talk with an ECK Spiritual Aide, a specially trained clergy member in Eckankar, who will mostly listen. The Master's direction often becomes clear during the ECK Spiritual Aide session.

The guiding rule that will stand you well throughout life is this ECK saying: Is it true, is it necessary, is it kind?

My spiritual insights:

A small night-light or two for your bedroom is a way to keep the powers of night at bay. Another is to have a pet in your room overnight. And keep up the spiritual exercises.

Some things I can do for myself for more peaceful sleep:

No two people are alike. Each has an agreement with life that is unlike any other. Learn love, patience, and grace, because they are the way to find harmony.

Finding peace is a big part of your spiritual life.

Age of High Sensitivity

I have a lot of trouble in my room. I am fourteen years old and still have nightmares or see things, such as a ghost. I do a visualization technique in which I put the ECK Masters around the windows and doors, but it doesn't always work. I still get afraid. What can I do?

You're at an age of high sensitivity. It can take the form of nightmares or seeing ghosts, a problem that my sister and I also ran into from about the age of twelve to fifteen.

A small night-light or two for your bedroom is a way to keep the powers of night at bay. Another is to have a pet in your room overnight. And keep up the spiritual exercises.

Don't watch horror shows on TV at all, but try to watch upbeat programs of comedy, nature, or sports. Many soft drinks are high in caffeine, which makes for tense nerves—so replace harmful soft drinks with herbal teas or fruit drinks. Take multivitamins and multiminerals. Be sure to get enough rest and exercise.

The above suggestions can bring you more calm. Put extra attention on peace and quiet for another year or two, after which your sensitivity will balance out.

Nightmares or Other Strange Things

Sometimes when I am playing alone, I look up and see someone I don't know. It isn't always the same person, but there are some I see more often than others.

I can make them go away if I close my eyes. Then when I open them again, they're gone.

I also sense if something bad is going to happen the next day, usually to someone I don't know. I don't know their names or exactly what will happen, but I know if they are a boy, girl, man, or woman. Then I hear something on the news about it. I also feel like someone is watching me from behind my back all the time. Are these things real or just my imagination? They make me feel afraid a lot of the time.

My mom tells me to sing HU, but even when I do, it feels like someone is right beside my face and I get scared and stop singing HU. What is happening to me, and how can I feel less afraid?

Are the things I see a gift from God, or are they illusions—my mind playing tricks on me?

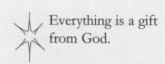

Everything is a gift from God.

Gifts from God in my life:

Everything is a gift from God. Please understand that even the Kal Niranjan is a servant of God and must answer to the ECK, the Voice of God. The Kal helps us face our weaknesses so that we may grow in strength.

Another thing to understand is illusion. The things of this world are real, but seen in a wrong light. People think that they're one thing when, in fact, there's more to them than meets the eye. It'd take pages to make the idea of illusion clearer to you. But let's just say they are real.

Now the challenge is to understand what is happening to you.

Young people your age are sometimes troubled by nightmares or other strange things. Their minds are still an open window to some past life when they trained as a priest or priestess to develop their powers of prophecy.

Some experiences I've had with love conquering fear:

This ability was the "second sight." It requires a strong person who won't be swept here and there by his emotions. But what to do?

Ask your parents to double-check your nutrition. Stop taking foods that stress the nerves like chocolate or soft drinks (often loaded with caffeine). Also cut down on the amount of other candies, and try fruit instead. Here, I may also suggest organic fruit, because regular fruit often has herbicides and pesticides on them.

Look also to the shows you watch on TV. Those with violence disturb the natural harmony of the emotional body.

Nor are computers the absolute boon to society that some claim, because the electricity sends out jagged waves that interrupt the normal nerve networks of sensitive people. Get enough sleep.

The Antidote for Fear

In my family the elder ones believe in supernatural things. For many years they made it clear to everyone in the family that some members of the family practiced witchcraft and had been controlling the family since its existence. Frankly, this planted deep seeds of fear in our consciousness. To make matters worse, the self-righteous ones accuse many members of the family of witchcraft.

First of all, is there such a person as a witch and does evil attack us in our family? Also, did it affect me and my immediate brothers and sisters? And what can I do to help solve the problems of my family?

Unfortunately, there is such a person as a witch. In fact, a witch is anyone who tries to control another by overt or hidden means.

Witchcraft is in every country. It is a practice employed by "good" members of a religious community who use force or guile to make others accept their beliefs. Needless to say, it is a spiritual violation.

What gives a witch power? Fear.

A culture that is saturated in a fear of supernatural things produces a people open to the power of witchcraft.

Beyond such a susceptibility, however, there is an inherent psychic power in witchcraft. It can have effects, or force, within the domain of the witch, be it a witch in the family, one next door, or in the neighborhood.

A simple answer, of course, is to leave such surroundings.

However, such an answer is simplistic. That is especially so when a victim has a duty to others in the family and must bear that responsibility. A witch trying to cast spells upon a chela (student) of the Mahanta, the Living ECK Master will, in time, come to grief.

The power of witchcraft will gradually die out in a strong community of ECK initiates.

Love for the Mahanta is the antidote for fear. This sweet love grows strong through the daily practice of the Spiritual Exercises of ECK.

Whenever you feel yourself under psychic attack by a witch, you can protect yourself. Sing HU, the love song to God, in silence, and fix your whole inner attention upon the loving radiance of the Mahanta. I am always with you.

Grow Spiritually by Meeting the Problem

Are there times when it is best not to do a spiritual exercise? When the negative energies in my life become

> Whenever you feel yourself under psychic attack, you can protect yourself. Sing HU, the love song to God.

A spiritual exercise I've tried:

What I experienced:

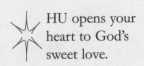

HU opens your heart to God's sweet love.

Ways I can be a model of love:

overwhelming, I try to stop what I am doing and do a short spiritual exercise.

But I wonder whether there are times when it would be better to just wait out the period of difficulty.

Keep doing the spiritual exercises, but do them in a different way.

People often get more intense with their exercises when things appear to go wrong. Why? Perhaps because they want to force something in their life to go where *they* feel it ought to go. Or, the going is tougher than they expected.

Do a spiritual exercise anyway when all goes wrong. However, do it with a new thought in mind. Say to the Mahanta, "What is thy will?" Then chant a sacred word, such as the name for God, HU. Put your full attention on the problem, for the Inner Master will show how you can grow spiritually by meeting the problem.

HU opens your heart to God, the ECK, and the Mahanta. In other words, it opens you to God's sweet love.

Parents Can Help You Learn

My parents make me study some things in Eckankar that I do not believe. What can I do about it? How can I let them know that I don't want to study certain things?

They probably also make you do some things you don't like apart from Eckankar.

No two people will ever see anything exactly alike. The problem can be worse in a home because it is like a pressure cooker. You and your parents have to live under the same roof and see each other every day.

As parents, they have the job of preparing you to be a responsible adult in today's society. For a while, my daughter and I had the same problem. She thought she could live any which way she pleased. I agreed but also told her there was a price to pay. Did she know what it was, and was she willing to pay it?

Most young people don't know the price. They need advice, but they don't want to get it from their parents. After all, their parents are the very ones from whom they are trying to win more freedom. This tension exists in nearly every family.

I have no single answer for you. If your parents are paying for the housing where you stay, then they have quite a bit to say about the rules of the house. Learn what you can from them. In the meantime, begin to plan for when you are of legal age and can have your own place. Read the classified ads and see what the cost of rentals is.

Then look in the classified ads again, this time in the Help Wanted section. See how much you'd need to earn to afford the kind of place you'd like to live in. Your parents can help you learn about the many costs involved in having your own place. Ask them about the cost of insurance, heating, and food. It may give you a common ground of understanding.

You may then find that you also have a lot in common about the teachings of Eckankar too. See if you can work something out.

Be the Model of Love

I am an ECKist who lives close to the ECK Temple of Golden Wisdom in Chanhassen, Minnesota. I get a lot of criticism at my school about my religion. People say that I worship the devil, that we (as ECKists) are Antichrists, that I am evil, and other negative rumors about the Temple of ECK that are even worse.

They don't ask me about these things, they tell me that they are real. Can you give me some insights on how to respond to these criticisms?

> Parents have the job of preparing you to be a responsible adult in today's society.

How my parents help me:

You'll gain strength from your experiences, for we make our own heavens.

My spiritual insights:

Hatred is a terrible thing. We know that the criticisms are false. Some people and their kids are not living up to the teachings of Christ.

Christ taught love, not hatred.

"Thou shalt love thy neighbour as thyself," he said. (So do they not love themselves that they hate you?) Christ called this quote the second commandment (Matt. 22:39).

Christ also said, "He that is without sin among you, let him first cast a stone at her" (John 8:7).

Again, he said, "Love your enemies," in Matt. 5:44.

Understand that the Law of Love applies to all. That includes ECKists. So your classmates break this Law of Love by their hatred of you. God will deal with them through the Lords of Karma, who impartially judge each action.

Don't be a sheep at school. You must be the model of love that Christ taught, even as all true masters teach their disciples to be carriers of love.

You must set a good example.

If you tell a classmate (who says false things about you) one of Christ's sayings above, he will catch himself. But only if that classmate is close to Christ's teachings. It could be that some only practice their religion in church on Sunday, but in their hearts are all the things they accuse you of.

It's tough. Perhaps you'll gain strength from your experiences, for we make our own heavens.

But don't be a rug for others' muddy feet either. If things get too rough at school, keep your parents up to speed. They may be able to help through other means.

Above all, chant HU silently when trouble comes at school. I am with you, you know.

Workbook:
How to Live and Make It in This World

Key Insights
from This Chapter

- Problems help us grow spiritually. Everything is a gift from God.

- Before taking an action, ask yourself: Is it true, is it necessary, is it kind?

- Be a model of divine love in any situation.

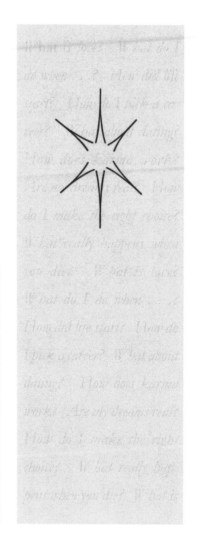

My key insights:

Spiritual Exercises to Explore These Insights

1. When a conflict arises at school, at home, or at your job, silently sing HU, the holy name of God. Sing it with love in your heart. This sacred sound can restore balance to your world and help you be a model of divine love.

    What happened when you did this? Write down your impressions and experiences here:

2. Whenever you have doubts about what to say in conversation or what action to take in a challenging situation, ask yourself these three questions:

- Is it true?

- Is it necessary?

- Is it kind?

How does this change what you say or do? Write what you discover here:

3. Practice looking for the spiritual lessons in the experiences you have this month. This will help you see how they are a gift from God to help you grow spiritually. Write your insights here:

Experience   **Spiritual lesson**

_____   _____

_____   _____

_____   _____

_____   _____

4. Both happy and unhappy experiences lead to Soul's purification. The key is to understand what is happening. Think of a challenge or problem you are facing. (You can ask the Inner Master for guidance, if you like.) Now, look at your life from the highest viewpoint; Soul has no limitations. What are three positive actions you can take to help resolve your problem? Write them below:

My challenge/problem is:

Positive actions I can take:

1.

2.

3.

5. You are Soul, here to learn spiritual lessons every day. What
    have you learned about yourself as you read this chapter?

The song of love
is sung through
respect and
thoughtfulness
for each other.

2

LOVE AND RELATIONSHIPS

What Kind of Relationship?

How does one know if a relationship is based on love and is worth developing?

No one has the final word on love, but consider the following points in deciding if you really love someone:

1. Does he bring joy to your heart when you think of him?
2. Do you want to make him happy?
3. Will you love him for what he is and not try to change him? Will you let him be as he is and not what you want him to be?
4. Young people tend to fall in love with their ideal of love. This means that one has the ideal of a Prince Charming who is really a toad. Not all Prince Charmings are toads, and not all toads are Prince Charmings.

> No one has the final word on love.

> Detached love means to let others exist without forcing our will upon them. That is spiritual love.

How I let my loved ones grow spiritually:

How they let me grow:

5. Don't forget your self-worth. How does he treat you—like a treasure or someone to be used?

Love is the expression of the ECK, Divine Spirit, on earth, and these points should give you a fairly good opportunity to see what kind of relationship you are in.

Spiritual Love

How can one have a healthy, loving relationship without getting too attached?

Not to get attached is often taken to mean "not to get involved." It actually means not to let your idea of how things should be dictate the relationship. That kind of love has strings attached. It means always trying to have your partner do what you think is right.

Those with pure love do all they can to let their mates grow in every way.

So we come to the real meaning of detached love. It means to let others exist without forcing our will upon them. That is spiritual love.

Little Things Count

As a youth, many gifts and acts of love have been given to me, especially from my parents. What are some ways that I can give this love back? In some families and societies, the parents take care of the youth, then when older, the youth take care of their parents. Should this be true to balance karmic ties, and is this true at all?

You have a good way of looking at the give-and-take of love.

Love shows itself in deeds of love. People who love people are the luckiest people in the world.

Real love is selfless. We do continual acts of kindness to make the way easier for our loved ones.

By giving love, we become magnets of love.

The happiest people I know are those who give and receive love from their families and friends. Now, we're talking about the "no-strings-attached" kind of love. We do chores around the home with cheerfulness. Of course, we have bad days. But love tries to keep those days in check.

How would you want others to treat you? Treat them the same way.

Spiritually healthy people like to be a ray of sunshine for the ones they love. So too will children, when grown, do what they can to ease the trials of aging for their parents. Little things count.

Count all the little everyday things your parents did for you as a child. Someday they'll need someone to do the same for them.

Yes, some families and societies have the practice of mutual care between parents and children at the different stages of life. Most people do so under the Law of Karma. That is just and right.

An ECKist, a member of Eckankar, though, acts in accord with a higher law, the Law of Love. It allows more joy and freedom for all members of the family.

Pets Teach about Life

What can pets teach us?

Not everybody owns a pet, or can. Some apartment managers won't allow them, nor can all parents afford them. But if you do have one, you'll find your pet a wonderful companion for teaching certain ways of the ECK (Holy Spirit).

There is an interesting book about how animals think and feel. *What the Animals Tell Me* by Beatrice

> Real love is selfless. We do continual acts of kindness to make the way easier for our loved ones.

Some acts of kindness I can do to make it easier for someone else:

To teach your pet obedience, try using sentences with only positive words in them.

Draw a picture of an animal or pet you love:

Lydecker tells how she learned to "talk" with her pets by using visualization methods.

Over the years, animals in Beatrice Lydecker's family included dogs, cats, cows, ducks, and other farm animals. The mental pictures she used to talk with them are like the visualization techniques explained by Paul Twitchell in the Eckankar book *The Flute of God*. Lydecker's methods of teaching animals are formed from spiritual wisdom, but her pets taught her a lot of lessons about life too.

The author once tried to teach her dog, Princessa, to speak. The author wanted the dog to bark for something it wanted. Hours passed as she prompted it by saying, "Woof, woof," but the dog sat in silence, a puzzled frown on its face.

Finally, she asked why it would not speak. By the inner language, it said, "You already know what I want. Why do I have to bark?"

In other experiments, she found that animals do not understand negative words, such as: *don't, can't, not, isn't, shouldn't,* and *wouldn't.* A dog that jumps on the bed and is ordered off with the command, "Don't go on the bed!" will probably stay on it. The pet drops the word *don't* and hears, "Go on the bed!" So it obeys, happy to please its master. Then it becomes confused when it is scolded for disobedience.

To teach your pet obedience, try using sentences with only positive words in them. First, visualize a picture in your mind of the dog on the floor beside the bed. Next, say, "Sit on the floor!" That command is a positive image and will work for most dogs in time.

What the Animals Tell Me gives sound tips for training pets. Anyone who is twelve or older should find the book easy to read. It is full of stories, examples, and tips on pet care centered on spiritual precepts. But the real message is between the lines: how you can open your eyes to the ECK.

The book may be in your local library. Call the librarian, and ask for it by title and the author's name. If it's not there, ask how you can find it.

If you don't have a pet of your own, make friends with cats and dogs near home. Then look at the world through their eyes, which is a Soul Travel exercise. You will see old things in a new light. Each time one sees with new eyes, he is nearer to being a Co-worker with God.

Dreams as Advisers

I have been having recurring dreams which involve me, my boyfriend, and another woman. In all the dreams, my boyfriend treats me like extra baggage and ignores me while paying attention to her.

We have been having difficulties in our relationship, and for some reason, I don't trust him. How can I tell whether my dreams are intuitive or simply represent my insecurities?

A relationship without trust won't last. What is the source of this mistrust? Does he look at other women when you are out together in public?

Dreams can prepare you for a relationship that may be coming to an end. They will tell you something is wrong. If your partner is showing less affection toward you, you must decide whether to try to patch up the relationship or let it go.

Think of your dreams as advisers. They may point out problems and offer solutions, but consider all the facts before deciding on any important issue. Especially watch people's daily behavior toward you. Your dreams may suggest what behavior to look out for, but don't break up a relationship without some physical evidence to back up your suspicions.

No matter what happens with this relationship, try to be a greater channel for divine love. Love will

Think of your dreams as advisers. They may point out problems and offer solutions, but consider all the facts before deciding on any important issue.

Something I've learned from a dream:

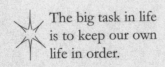

The big task in life is to keep our own life in order.

What I can do to keep my life in order:

overcome suspicion, which can destroy any relationship.

Right Living Includes Right Discrimination

My older brother has been struggling for as long as I can remember with his spiritual path and himself. I see God giving him many gifts and experiences that he is blindly passing by.

I feel so helpless. I love him deeply, and I see how he hurts inside. What can I do to help him become happier with himself? Is there anything I can do to help him realize the experiences he goes through are great gifts that can guide him in the right direction?

Perhaps the hardest thing we face is seeing a loved one spurn life's blessings and choose the low road.

You'll see such behavior as long as you live. All you can do is to give people like that your love, but not in a blind way. For example, if someone wants to harm himself with alcoholic drinks, illegal drugs, or even the purchases of material goods far beyond his means to afford them, think twice about being the moneybags.

So what's the issue here, his life or yours?

Right living also includes right discrimination. That boils down to having a command of our emotions. When a loved one chooses to walk the path of self-destruction, the choice is ours of how far we'll accompany him. That path will harm us too.

The big task in life is to keep our own life in order. That means controlling our runaway emotions, for unless we do, the misguided steps of others will wreck our emotions.

It gets down to your choice. Will you let your older brother ruin both your lives? Keep in mind that the world is full of self-destructive people, but don't be a magnet for them. It's like trying to be a world savior. Adults are responsible for their own lives and must accept the consequences of their actions.

Yes, this is hard love. I wish this could be a gentler answer, but life teaches many lessons through the deeds of others.

That lets us know that mud is dirty without soiling our own clothes.

Control of Anger

I argue all the time with myself and my family. I've tried exercises and positive thoughts, but I keep on arguing anyway. What should I do?

We get into arguments because we don't like the rules put on us. We feel that somebody has put us in a prison and there is no way out.

You are in your family because it is the best place for you to learn the customs of society. This sort of discipline gets you ready for the next level of growth and freedom. The ECK, the Holy Spirit, won't let us take shortcuts if it would hurt us. We get just the right experience, and not a bit more.

To get in control of your anger, try to catch yourself in the middle of an argument. Then chant HU, the holy name for God, softly to yourself.

Let the argument run its natural course, just to see what it does to you. Suddenly you are surprised to find you are now in control of whether to argue or not, instead of being a helpless victim of your mind. Try this, and see how it works.

What to Look for in a Date

Is there a difference between dating a person on my spiritual path and someone who is not?

To get in control of your anger, try to catch yourself in the middle of an argument. Then chant HU softly to yourself.

Ways I can control my anger:

The song of love is sung through respect and thoughtfulness for each other. They are the best assurance of a gracious and loving bond for years to come.

Write a song of love or a love note that shows your respect and thoughtfulness to someone:

The best answer is a question: Are two different Souls the same?

Naturally, not. What, then, does someone following a spiritual path such as Eckankar look for in a date? Can you respect her beliefs and feelings? Does she respect yours? Are you a better, happier person in her company?

A light friendship is fairly easy to deal with, but when a special woman brings thoughts of marriage or a lasting relationship, look carefully at her family, her education, her plans for a family, her housekeeping habits, her handling of money. Are they like yours?

New love overlooks a lot of shortcomings, like a partner who spends more than she earns. But what happens when the debts pile up and a baby is suddenly on the way? Where is the money for doctor bills? Problems like these can make for two very unhappy people.

No matter how great your love for each other, things will always tug at its seams. The song of love is sung through respect and thoughtfulness for each other. They are the best assurance of a gracious and loving bond for years to come.

Finding Balance with Others

How do I balance what I want and still leave other people their freedom? Especially when my desires involve others?

Let's say a person wanted companionship. He might put the request to Divine Spirit, then do those things out here that he had to do to get ready—shave, dress nicely, whatever. Then he would leave the results to Spirit.

But if the person directs his request, saying, "That is the person I would like to share my life with,"

maybe his desire is not part of that other person's life scheme. He'll probably find that what he imagines won't come true. It gets into the freedom of another individual.

When you don't put a definite shape to what you imagine, Divine Spirit can have unlimited freedom to fill that mold. But if you put a limit to it, you often strike out because you've allowed for only one possible outcome.

Sex and Spirituality

What is the connection between spirituality and sex?

The deep relationship between man and woman is a sacred token of human love. The sex urge does not lift anyone into the higher heavens, so why endorse sex as a means for spiritual unfoldment?

This relationship between a couple must be open and clean, without guilt or shame. If you cannot love your family, how will you then love God? The dirt and guilt that the orthodox religions put upon lovemaking is for control of the followers. Guilt and fear have been deeply impressed upon them for centuries.

Lovemaking, a deep expression of love and warmth between a man and a woman, is their private business. Overindulgence in anything is lust. Will we be pulled down to the common level of the animal?

The union between man and woman demands mutual responsibility. The ECK Masters advocate virginity until marriage, but I do not intrude into your private life to judge your personal relationships.

Homosexuality

I would like to know the implications of homosexuality from the spiritual viewpoint. I cannot speak to

When you don't put a definite shape to what you imagine, Divine Spirit can have unlimited freedom to fill that mold.

My spiritual insights:

The ECK, or Holy
Spirit, begins
uplifting Soul
from Its present state
into higher ones.

Ways I was uplifted
today:

anyone about it. I wonder if homosexuality affects spiritual unfoldment.

Thank you for your letter regarding homosexuality and living the life of ECK. Your personal life is for you to choose.

The ECK, or Holy Spirit, begins uplifting Soul from Its present state into higher ones. As this happens, those practices which are obstacles on your next step to Self- and God-Realization will dissolve through the purification given by the ECK.

Whatever one does in his personal affairs is a matter solely between Divine Spirit and himself. The Living ECK Master wants to direct Soul to Its true home in the Ocean of Love and Mercy. He has no interest in social issues or reform, only in the preservation of the individual throughout eternity.

Spiritual Twins

What is meant by the term spiritual twin *as mentioned in the Eckankar book* The ECK-Vidya, Ancient Science of Prophecy, *by Paul Twitchell?*

It does not refer to Soul mates, or time twins.

That old idea rests upon a lesser line of affinity that can exist between two people. It may include such things as physical appearance, a common interest in a social cause, or even be a chemical bond between two people.

These values are of the Kal, or negative in nature.

Spiritual twins are something else. They are two people who each want the ECK (Holy Spirit) more than anything else in life. And they help each other reach It. In time, the male and female forces within each come into harmony, as they reach the Soul Plane and become the ECK Itself.

That is love at its finest.

Gaining Discrimination

A male friend seemed to be a perfect match for me. Whenever we were together a tremendous flow of energy came through; he said being with me allowed him to travel to higher spiritual levels. Now as I look back I wonder if he was using me. I trusted him so much that I looked beyond his lies and unsanitary lifestyle, thinking it was a test for me. How can I judge situations like this in the future?

In matters of the heart, trust your common sense. Only you can decide whether any relationship is for your growth or not. I certainly do not endorse people who use the ECK teachings to get into bed with someone. Since that is a personal relationship between two consenting adults, it is outside the realm of my suggestions.

To give understanding in the future, the act of lovemaking does not raise anyone much beyond the astral, or emotional, level of consciousness, and certainly not to the high levels of heaven. Thus Eckankar will never become a sex cult.

A rule of thumb is that a person's state of consciousness can be perceived somewhat by his cleanliness. Every clean person is not necessarily a highly unfolded being, but it certainly is true that no spiritually evolved individual is habitually dirty or slovenly.

Do not fall for the trap of guilt or self-condemnation, but rely on common sense.

What Am I Doing Wrong?

I am continually amazed at how hard life is for me. I am, frankly, questioning God's system—it seems too difficult. I have used all kinds of spiritual techniques, and I am still perplexed.

> In matters of the heart, trust your common sense. Only you can decide whether any relationship is for your growth or not.

How I am learning to trust my heart *and* my common sense:

There is a gap between what you think you're getting and what you finally end up with.

It centers on my personal relationships. I attract men who desire other women, even in the throes of the greatest love. No man seems to be able to love the way I am able to. What am I doing wrong to be so unhappy?

If everybody had the deep problems you have, I'd be forced to say, "Yes, God's plan for the unfoldment of Soul is impractical and unworkable." But very few people who write to me have the ongoing life of misery that you report.

By all accounts, you are an attractive, desirable individual. Yet in your personal relationships, you continually find yourself in the most unhappy circumstances. Let's see if we can shed light on the reasons for this.

As a personal study, have you ever put the names of all the important men in your life on a single piece of paper, with two categories under each: *attractions* and *final weak points*? In other words, what about each man attracted you to him. Be both honest and fair.

Then look at each of the men to see what it was about them in particular that caused a parting. There is a gap between what you think you're getting and what you finally end up with. You want to close the gap between illusion and reality *before* you invest too much heartache in the relationship.

I've known people with the uncanny ability to choose three alcoholic mates in a row. Maybe it wasn't so surprising since they looked for companions in drinking establishments. Not one of these people realized they were always fishing in the same water, using the same bait. No wonder they kept coming up with the same kind of fish.

To turn around a life that's so often upside down, the individual must first make an honest inventory of all the factors that have caused the trouble. It's too easy to blame something outside of us for our troubles, especially if we do not like what we see in ourselves. But fixing the blame elsewhere will not make the trouble go away.

First make the list of all the men in your life, with their qualities of initial attraction for you. In that should be a clue why your relationships always end up wrong. Don't forget *where* you met them. What mutual interests drew you together? Did those same interests rebound on you to destroy the very relationship they helped to create?

Please be objective in your analysis of the men in your life. Otherwise you're no better off than when you started. You are a loving, giving individual. Now you must learn to find someone who is worthy of that love.

When you finish the list of the men, take another sheet and write "Arguments" at the top of it. Again list the same men. Try to put down the things you and each man mostly argued about. Besides outside relationships, were any of the arguments about money? List all of the subjects of disagreement with each man. That list should tell you something about yourself.

The answers you come up with on your list can help you see the next step in changing the conditions of your thought so that old patterns of the past can be broken and give you a fresh promise of a better future.

Cultural Karma

Growing up in Eckankar, I learned to love and view all people as Soul. Why do my parents object to my interracial relationship?

Sometimes parents are pointing out the extra cultural karma that their offspring may inadvertently

> To turn around a life that's so often upside down, the individual must first make an honest inventory of all the factors.

Old thoughts I'd like to change:

New thoughts I'd like to have:

> Society puts restraints on us until we learn what consequences we will shoulder for certain actions.

What spiritual exercise helps me make better decisions?

take on in addition to the personal, family, and other karma that is part of any love relationship. Their opinion is to be considered carefully, of course, but the final decision is yours.

Everything depends upon the people, time, and place. If those three parts go against what a society accepts as normal, then members of that society will make life rough for the couple.

Let's draw a picture of an extreme case for you. Consider this: two people of the same sex *and* of mixed races who expect all the legal rights of a couple of opposite sexes. They would have a lot of problems in many parts of the world today. In a lesser way, a heterosexual couple of mixed races would have more problems in a lot of places than would a similar couple of the same race.

Weigh the odds and do as you please. It all adds to your spiritual unfoldment if you love one another.

Virginity

You've stated that while it is up to the individual, the ECK Masters advocate chastity or virginity until marriage. Can you please explain why such a life is suggested?

First of all, it *is* a suggestion, not an order. A young person is in intensive training the first eighteen or more years of his life, learning the responsibility of self-discipline that is needed for him to be self-supporting in the world.

There is a time and a place for everything. It is natural for us to chafe against the rules that hinder our freedom. But society puts restraints on us until we learn what consequences we will shoulder for certain actions. Ignorance is no excuse under the Law of Karma.

When one is an infant, he is often a self-centered, selfish person. Because he is helpless, he is used to the world catering to his whims. All the baby has to do is cry or whine to get attention. Of course, sometime between infancy and adulthood, the individual learns that he's got the workings of the world backward: He is to serve life; life does not serve him. Until this lesson hits home, he is not understanding the purpose of Soul's reincarnation, which is to become a Co-worker with God.

Virginity is suggested for the youth because without a fair grounding in life, an individual is hollow inside and mistakes sex for love. Sex takes, love gives. Unless there is love, life can be a miserable and sad experience: an unnecessary detour on the road to God.

Also, consider this: How can a child raise a child?

People of every society have rules of conduct. These rules say what is right or wrong in that society. Men, women, and children are to obey its rules for the sake of order. The ECK Masters uphold all just laws.

Let's look at a child in society. The child must first learn to care for itself. Today, that often means learning to read and write, do simple chores, make meals, and to clean up after oneself. Later, it also means finding a job.

A baby starts life with no skills at all. It begins to pick up some easy skills as a child, and the harder ones come later when it is a young adult. The harder skills are learning to get along with others, even when you don't get your way.

Being born means having to learn to care for ourselves in a society. Each of us must learn how.

But could a ten-year-old girl raise a baby in most parts of the world? I think not, because the girl is herself a child. At what age would she be a good mother? And when does a boy become a man, fit for

> Being born means having to learn to care for ourselves in a society. Each of us must learn how.

Ways I care for myself:

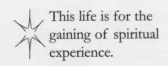 This life is for the gaining of spiritual experience.

Some of my favorite spiritual experiences:

the duties of being a father? Is it ten, fifteen, or what? Each society has its own rules about that.

So your question is really about being a mature person in society.

Life Partners

How important is it to date or marry someone in the same religion as me?

This life is for the gaining of spiritual experience.

Life partners often—nearly always—reach an agreement with others important to their mutual spiritual unfoldment long before either of them becomes aware of it on earth. But destiny is not fixed. Each has to find the other, often sorting through many possible choices.

An ECKist will, of course, consider both ECKists and non-ECKists as a life partner. Most Souls agree to total amnesia before their return to earth in new bodies. The reason for that is to avoid old biases and hatreds. Amnesia gives one a fresh start.

Your spirituality depends upon yourself. Someone in your religion may or may not be the right choice for you at a given time, so look around. Ask the Mahanta, the Inner Master, to help you weigh the spiritual advantages of each potential life partner.

Talking with Wah Z

When I go into my dreams and have an experience with the Mahanta, what should I say to him?

You'll know exactly what to say.

Who is your best friend at school? Is it hard to speak to a friend, your parents, or a brother or sister? Of course not. Talking with Wah Z (my spiritual name as the Inner Master) is the same thing.

By the time you meet Wah Z, you will know him as a dear friend of old. This is not your first lifetime, you know. Like everyone else, you've spent so many lifetimes bumping around in spiritual darkness.

Say you're in your home and the electricity goes off. Dark, scary, and lonesome? You bet.

But then you see the bobbing light of a flashlight coming from somewhere, cutting through the curtain of darkness. How do you feel? You get a sudden feeling of relief. Someone's bringing a light.

The Mahanta brings you a light too.

One other point to keep in mind: As above, so below. It means that everything first happens above, on one of the higher spiritual planes: Astral, Causal, etc. So if you're in an ECK family and know of the Mahanta, you've earned the right to meet him.

Now it's simply a matter of remembering.

The surest way to remember what happens when we see each other in the dream worlds is by doing one of the many Spiritual Exercises of ECK.

Yes, we know each other and have for a long time. Long before you came to this world.

Friends help each other, or what are friends for? Call on Wah Z any time. OK?

What Is True Marriage?

What does the marriage bond signify spiritually?

The marriage bond can only be sacred if it is sacred to the two individuals who have agreed to this union. If they are one in heart, how can they be divided? At their marriage, one couple in Eckankar made a "first cause" statement to each other. They each made a vow to help the other become an ECK Master in this lifetime. They would help each

> The surest way to remember what happens when we see each other in the dream worlds is by doing one of the many Spiritual Exercises of ECK.

Things I want to talk to the Inner Master about:

other in conscious spiritual evolution, out of love, to reach the heights of God.

A true marriage has commitment by each person. Both realize the responsibility of that commitment. A marriage of the heart lets each of the couple remain an individual, but the two are as one.

When Your Parents Divorce

How can people find out whether they love truly or not, and why are they hasty to get married? Why do I find myself in my family instead of another family, and what can a child do to keep from suffering so much when their parents divorce?

Love is blind and probably always will be. The only way to find out anything in life is to go ahead and get the experience. Nothing is ever lost. Each experience can teach us valuable lessons about ourselves, painful though they may be.

Impatience and blindness (a lack of experience in such matters) are the reason for hasty marriages. There's little that can be done about it.

Why are you in your family and not another? It's for the simple reason that you and your parents agreed to it before this lifetime ever began. Somehow, all of you saw a spiritual reason for being together. So in contemplation ask the Mahanta to show you in some way what some of those reasons were. It will make you a person of more love, wisdom, and compassion.

How to keep from suffering so much when parents divorce? Love the parent you're with, with all your heart. In other words, fill yourself with love for all who are with you now, this minute, this hour.

Give love, love, and even more love. And know that I am always with you. Because I am.

Fill yourself with love for all who are with you now, this minute, this hour. Give love, love, and even more love.

Write ways you can love your parents or family more:

Power of Love

In the Eckankar book Stranger by the River, *by Paul Twitchell, what does it mean when the Tibetan ECK Master Rebazar Tarzs says that a woman's heart is the throne of God on earth?*

The chapter is called "The Great Tree of Life." Read it very carefully again, from beginning to end. Rebazar Tarzs is comparing a life full of love to one without it.

Look especially at the paragraph before that, where he speaks of beauty. It is the harmony between joy and pain that begins in the body but ends beyond the mind. Beauty is "the power which leads man's heart to that of a woman, which is, on this earth, the throne of God."

Throne here means the source of divine love.

But Rebazar goes on, and what he says now is highly important, for it explains where true love begins and what conditions the lover must meet.

Love, says Rebazar, is "that holy liquor which God has wrung from His great heart and poured into the lover's heart for his beloved." Notice also the hint that not everyone can drink of this holy love, because the lover must meet a set condition: purity of heart. "He who can drink this liquor is pure and divine, and his heart has been cleansed of all but pure love!" That means, among other things, a lack of selfishness.

Next, he speaks of the power of love in very powerful language: "Thus I say that the lover whose heart is drunk with love is drunk with God."

But Rebazar goes a step further. Love does not begin and end with one's love for his beloved, but it will of its own accord flow out to embrace all life. So his message is this: Open your heart to love, for it can help you reach the fullest satisfaction in life, with all its joy and pain. "Let this be thy understanding in Eckankar," he adds. "Share thy cup with thy beloved,

> Love does not begin and end with one's love for his beloved, but it will of its own accord flow out to embrace all life.

How can I be more loving?

and never fail to help thine own in pain and suffering. This should be thy law unto thyself, my son."

A final word: When Rebazar here speaks of man and woman he doesn't only mean male and female, but the plus and minus sides of a human being. His message is about the power of love. This divine power can touch the heart in many ways, and love between a man and a woman is simply one of them.

I know this is a long reply, but perhaps it can point you toward a richer and happier life.

Love Is All There Is

I'm not sure what it means to really love God. How can I develop a loving relationship with God?

Put your attention upon divine love. Put your love into the things you do. Give your love to your dear ones.

Love is all there is. It is the beginning and end of life. Ask the Mahanta to guide you in the ways of God's love, and life will bring you every experience needed. That is the easy way.

In time, divine love will take you to the top of the spiritual mountain. There, you will experience the wonders of Self- and God-Realization in the proper seasons of your life. And, in the end, you will love God completely.

Human Love and Divine Love

What is human love and what is divine love? How can I learn to live divine love?

You want to know the difference between love and divine love. Begin with love, and that grows into divine love. I know that's not the answer you look for, but the mind has nothing to do with love.

> Divine love will take you to the top of the spiritual mountain. There, you will experience the wonders of Self- and God-Realization in the proper seasons of your life.

Ask the Inner Master to help you find out more about love. Write what you learn:

Begin with the love you have. Love gratefully. This love expands your heart into a greater vessel which can hold yet more love. On the outside, divine and emotional love may look the same, but divine love is joyful, thankful. It gives itself fully.

Let love be what it will. Don't let the mind tell you one is human and the other divine. Just love without expecting its return.

Loving Yourself

On the path to Self-Realization, how can Soul go about learning to love Itself?

Love others more. Then, loving yourself just happens.

Pure Love

What is the difference between the love one has for one's mate and the love Soul has for God?

Is one sort of love better than the other? And is it still possible to fall in love with someone after you reach God Consciousness?

The highest love is a pure love for God.

A pure love for one's mate is the same as a pure love for God. There is no difference. But, frankly, pure love is a rarity—whether for God or for mate.

"Falling in love" usually means falling into karma. Karma—good, bad, or neutral—sets the tone for a relationship. For example, some couples love to fight.

The attraction between people of a high state of consciousness is a mutual desire to serve God and life. Such a couple join forces to help each other reach even higher states of being.

A high, pure love is sweet indeed.

Begin with the love you have. Love gratefully. This love expands your heart into a greater vessel which can hold yet more love.

Ways to love gratefully:

Workbook:
Love and Relationships

Key Insights
from This Chapter

- Love gratefully. This love expands your heart into a greater vessel which can hold yet more love.

- Love shows itself in deeds of love.

- The highest love is a pure love for God.

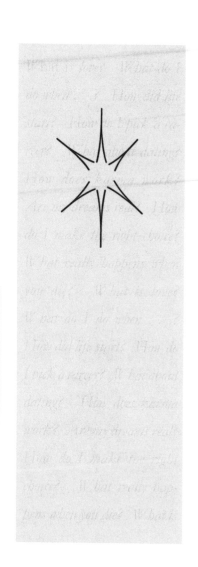

My key insights:

Spiritual Exercises to Explore These Insights

1. Cut out magazine pictures or words that describe your ideal relationship, one that expresses a grateful love that expands your heart. You can make a scrapbook on what love means to you or answer these questions in your journal or the space below: If you could imagine having the best relationship, what would it look like? What spiritual qualities would you choose to have in your family, with friends, with a boyfriend or girlfriend?

2. If you are not sure if a relationship is worth developing or if you really love someone, ask yourself these questions:

   - Does this person bring joy to my heart when I think of him or her?

   - Do I want to make him or her happy?

   - Will I love this person for what he is and not try to change him?

   - Will I let her be as she is and not what I want her to be?

   And don't forget your self-worth. How does this person treat you—like a treasure or someone to be used?

3. If you have a relationship challenge, think of how an ECK
   Master would solve it. Another way to do this is to ask, What
   would love do? Ask inwardly for three loving actions you could
   take to solve your problem, that would come from the Soul point
   of view.

   Write them here:

1.

2.

3.

4. Try one of the above three loving actions. Write your insights
   here:

Find a quiet place and focus within. Ask to be guided in the
ways of God's love, so life will bring you every experience you
need. What did you learn?

5. You are Soul, here to learn spiritual lessons every day. What
    have you learned about yourself as you read this chapter?

Do everything, large or small, as if you were doing it for God—with love, joy, and thoroughness.

3

CHANGE AND GROWTH

Your Spiritual Growth

What is the ultimate goal of Soul?

Here is a brief review of the final goal of Soul: It gathers an education in the lower worlds so that It can become a true citizen in the spiritual community. This is what we call a Co-worker with God.

The relationship between parent and child in the worlds of matter is based upon this spiritual design. The parent is the vehicle for the child's entrance into the world and is responsible for his education. The child must, between birth and the age of perhaps eighteen, learn all the dos and don'ts of his culture. The significant fact underlying the parent-child relationship is that there is more freedom for the child as he gets older and assumes more responsibility. The parent has failed his duties if the child reaches legal age and is unfit to take his place in the world.

Soul gathers an education in the lower worlds so that It can become a true citizen in the spiritual community.

The path of Eckankar encourages the freedom and responsibility of Soul. After all, that is Its birthright.

Every Soul is a spark of God. The child learns by making errors, but the wise parent must let the child learn for himself, giving guidance when it is necessary.

Why Are We Here?

In the grand scheme of things, why are we here? I believe I understand that we are here to attain Self-Realization, then later God-Realization on our journey home to God to truly be a Co-worker. Why this "journey" in the first place?

Why this journey home to God?

Do you know the parable of the prodigal son? A young man, born into all the advantages of a wealthy family, decided to leave home and see the world. Well, he wasted his money and ended up in a far land, among strangers, working as a swineherd. He would gladly have eaten what the pigs did.

One day it came to him: here he was living nearly like a beggar. Even his father's hired servants fared better.

So the wastrel returned home.

"Father," he said, "I'm a waste. I'm not worthy to be called your son. Make me as one of your servants."

But his father greeted him with joy and dressed him in the finest clothes. Further, his father made up a feast in celebration of his son's return home.

A beautiful story once told by Christ. He, like all true avatars, told people of their divine heritage. And so do we.

The journey to God is a journey back home to God. The high heavens are the true home of Soul. It is in

---

The path of Eckankar encourages the freedom and responsibility of Soul. After all, that is Its birthright.

What am I responsible for in my life?

How am I free because of this?

exile in these lower worlds of time, space, and matter to learn the lessons of humility and love. Like the prodigal son.

On earth, the common state of awareness is the human consciousness. As one learns more about love and humility through the trials of many lifetimes, he moves higher in consciousness. First comes cosmic consciousness. Later, for one in ECK, Self- and Spiritual Realization.

The highest level comes to the few who love and serve God with their whole being—God-Realization. It's a state of wonder and bliss beyond words. It's Soul's destiny.

Now you know the story.

Getting Inner Answers with the Easy Way Technique

What's the best way to work on the inner to get answers to spiritual questions?

A good way to start is with an ECK spiritual exercise known as the Easy Way technique.

Just before going to bed at night place your attention on the Spiritual Eye, that place between the eyebrows. Chant HU or God inwardly and silently.

Hold your attention on a blank screen in the inner vision, and keep it free of any pictures if at all possible. If you need a substitute for mental pictures flashing up unwantedly, put the image of the Living ECK Master in place of them.

Do this spiritual exercise for fifteen or twenty minutes a day. It generally won't happen overnight, but when the time is right, you will begin to see lights, usually blue or white. You will then be led to the next step within your own worlds.

The Easy Way technique is an opportunity in learning to rely on the Inner Master. Mentally ask

> Just before going to bed at night place your attention on the Spiritual Eye, that place between the eyebrows. Chant HU or God inwardly and silently.

> Try the Easy Way technique. What did you experience?

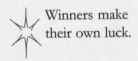 Winners make their own luck.

Think of something you want to do and make a plan:

your question while you're doing the Easy Way technique and again ask it before dropping off to sleep at night. The answer will come, sometimes in an obvious manner. Other times it comes subtly—through the advice of a friend, a humorous anecdote, or as a symbolic dream that you develop the knack of interpreting for yourself.

List all your questions on a sheet of paper. A month later, review them to see if any have resolved themselves. Do this with all your questions every month. You can send a report to me, if you like, regarding the results.

Catch the Right Wave

I realize that some people—including myself at times—want to believe in chance so as to evade personal responsibility. Yet even when we're ready and willing to accept responsibility for our thoughts, words, and deeds, it does seem that we still have to "catch the right wave" before we achieve success in our endeavors. Can you please shed some light on this?

To "catch the right wave." Fortune has a habit of finding those who can make a plan and stick with it. True, one person out of a million hits the big time by winning the lottery, but don't plan your fortune or future by simply buying lottery tickets week after week.

Winners make their own luck.

Many people who deal with failure have the peculiar habit of self-destruction. For example, a student may study moderately hard nearly the whole school term, yet then neglect to study for the final exam. Or even worse, not show up at all. Why?

The first step to finding success is being true to yourself and others.

Simple English, please?

Do everything, large or small, as if you were doing it for God alone. That means the task will be done with love, joy, and (don't forget) thoroughness.

Success is a little like heaven: There's always another step. A corollary of that idea is that success comes about in steps. And a plan simply creates those steps in the imagination, then on paper, then in reality.

You have a fine mind. Use it wisely to help you find success.

Facing Responsibilities

Decisions await me about how to handle responsibilities—either in career or college, or in personal relationships. I see responsibility as another face of love. But is there a way to tell if I'm using responsibility as an excuse to avoid experiences?

Responsibility is a big word, and it can frighten us. It tries to take a snapshot of us running through life and put a caption to this single picture, which is so small compared to all life that it's nearly invisible.

But what does a word like that tagged on to what we do after it's done mean? As you say, responsibility is another face of love. Every time a decision faces you, the question is: Will you be responsible or not? But responsible to whom?

The usual definition of responsibility is what society expects of you, but that may not always be the right thing to do. At the crossroads of decision, ask the Mahanta, the Inner Master, what to do. He will tell you by intuition, by knowing, or by direct speech, what decision is spiritually correct.

Do everything, large or small, as if you were doing it for God alone.

Ways I show responsibility:

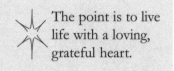

The point is to live life with a loving, grateful heart.

Ways I live life with a grateful heart:

For now, get experiences in work, in education, in your spiritual exercises, and in your personal relationships. When you turn decisions over to the Mahanta, this expression of the Spirit of God that is always with you, you will do the responsible thing. The point is to live life with a loving, grateful heart.

Why Are You in This Situation?

I find myself in an awkward situation. Leaders I admire for their successes and initiation level are using so-called love and their spiritual status to control me.

The control is so subtle that it is hard to see. I am supposed to believe that their spiritual experiences are bigger than mine or that their spiritual connection is greater than mine so I should listen to them and do things the way they want me to.

Love is given to me, but it comes with strings attached. How do I know when someone is trying to manipulate my energy and attention for their gain? And once I really know, as Soul, that this is happening, how do I deal with it?

By writing down this question so clearly, it shows that you, as Soul, already know that someone is trying to manipulate your energy and attention for their gain.

So let's go to the second question.

In contemplation, ask the Mahanta to show you what *you* are gaining from such an involvement. It couldn't exist without some sort of a mutual benefit. At one time, when you let such people into your personal life, the benefit to both sides was in balance. But now you are on the short end. That's why you're unhappy.

First, try to see what has changed. If the problems weigh more than the benefits, ask the Mahanta to show the best way to unwind your involvement with grace and goodwill. That is the second, most important part.

This is a spiritual lesson in self-responsibility. It will make you stronger. More loving.

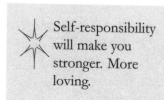

Self-responsibility will make you stronger. More loving.

Helping Adults Accept Change

What is absolutely the hardest thing you have to do?

Helping adults accept a change for something spiritually better. Doing new things is quite natural for young people. They're always growing out of clothes, so they get used to buying new things in a larger size.

Adults normally have fewer changes. They stopped growing years ago. In fact, some adults tend to hang on to an image of themselves as youths. But the 1920s, and even the 1970s, are long gone.

Most people can accept new developments of science like TV, the calculator, and the personal computer. These products can help them to become unstuck from their old ways of thinking. Science has transformed the way we do things.

Yet now people are too busy with scientific gadgets to bother about learning Soul Travel. But some individuals in the crowd will always desire truth more than anything else. It is for them that the Living ECK Master agrees to serve mankind.

How Our Lessons Come

As a guitar player, I really want to go way out there and bring back the music that moves and inspires people. I also want to be unique and not copy anyone. So how can I go deeper into my music?

To play that sort of music, you need to know people. How do you do that?

Ways self-responsibility makes me stronger and more loving:

Divine Spirit often gives the most valuable lessons in a simple job, like dish washing. Learn to care for yourself first, for only then can you reach and serve others.

Be among them; work and live as they do. Not in some idle way, as an idyllic troubadour—unless that is how you earn a living. A key phrase here is "earn a living."

Life teaches us best through our misfortunes.

Don't look for them, but do learn to take care of yourself. Divine Spirit often gives the most valuable lessons in a simple job, like dish washing. Learn to care for yourself first, for only then can you reach and serve others. That's true for a musician or anyone else.

And do the Spiritual Exercises of ECK every day.

Which way am I going in my life?

Spiritual Unfoldment: Move Forward, Backward, or Stand Still

What if, as a child, you forgot your special word for contemplation? How do you find another one? And why are they so important? Isn't HU good enough? Also, what do you do if spiritual exercises just don't work or have the same effect as they used to, or if concentration is nearly impossible for some reason? And why does this happen?

Lots of questions. All are answered elsewhere in the ECK teachings. But here's a short version: *How to find another special word?*

The answer is in your contemplations. In some way, at some time, the Mahanta will give it to you either in a dream, by intuition, or in your waking outer life. Be open to all possible words. Try one new one at a time during each spiritual exercise.

And by all means, flip through *A Cosmic Sea of Words: The ECKANKAR Lexicon* for new ideas. When a word stands out, experiment with it.

Yes, HU is good enough.

All sounds and, indeed, all words derive from it. A special word gives focus to some particular aspect of your spiritual unfoldment. For example, walking is a good general exercise. But if you'd like to develop more grace, a rhythmic dance would serve you better.

No spiritual exercise will always work the way it used to.

Things change. After all, isn't change the very nature of life? Nothing is ever the same. A lesson learned early or late in the ECK teachings is that Soul can go in one of three ways in any stage of Its spiritual unfoldment. It can move forward, backward, or stand still. That's it.

Why is concentration nearly impossible at times?

Here individuals must look at their own discipline. The mind is a restless creation, like a disobedient or destructive child. Soul, like a good parent, must bring it into line. And the sooner the better. The longer a bad habit is allowed free rein, the more unruly it becomes.

Your questions are good ones. I hope these answers give you a better spiritual understanding.

Lessons on Paying Attention

I had a camera stolen from me in Europe, and I was wondering why this sort of thing happens. Is it just because I'm not paying attention or is there some deeper karma involved?

The karma here was simply about learning to pay attention. If something is valuable to you—a camera, a loved one, a state of mind—it pays not to neglect it.

In the future, no doubt, you'll pay special attention to any new camera because you still feel the pain of loss from your old one. The loss of a camera is a cheap lesson if it gets across the lesson of being careful with those things that have a special value for us.

Precious is as precious does.

> Soul can go in one of three ways in any stage of Its spiritual unfoldment. It can move forward, backward, or stand still.

How can I move forward?

It sometimes takes time for a friendship, a relationship, to right itself after a new spice is tossed into the pot.

What I am learning from my friends:

Disagreement on Religion

One of my friends recently converted to Christianity, and I'm afraid this will deeply affect our relationship. I was always able to talk to her about religion before. All of my other Christian friends preach to me. As a result, I lose a close bond. Should I be concerned with such a change between me and my best friend?

These are among what could be either pleasant or uncomfortable changes in our lives. There are Christians and there are Christians. Just like ECKists.

Nobody with any degree of self-respect likes to be preached at, ECKist or Christian.

If she's really a good friend, her conversion will not stand in the way of your friendship. The first time a disagreement comes up between you on religion, say, "It's time we talk."

There is a saying, "Don't discuss politics or religion with friends unless they think like you." So agree on that.

Now remember, preaching at someone cuts both ways. Some ECKists make terrible pests of themselves at times too. Sad to say, in my exuberance at finding the ECK teachings years ago, I also plagued others with my excitement. No harm meant, but surely done. Of course, I paid dearly for that until it finally sunk in to keep my mouth shut.

There's no reason to cry over spilled milk. It's the way of Soul's education here. The players in our life *will* include our best friends. How else could it be?

Some people are born with grace, wisdom, and a good measure of diplomacy. They can handle problems such as yours so that a friendship need not explode in your hands. There is a way to be gracious. It sometimes takes time for a friendship, a relationship, to right itself after a new spice is tossed into the pot.

Though other "friends" may fail you, the Mahanta is always true.

Evolution

Can you explain evolution?

Evolution is a guess by science about how a life-form changed since its beginning. A key word is *change.*

Evolution is the idea that everything changes over time. One example is the family of elephants, which includes the mammoth of thousands of years ago. The mammoth and the elephant came from the same ancestor. Today the mammoth is gone, and the elephant remains.

Change is natural. So evolution fits right in with the Eckankar teachings.

Life's Many Crossroads

I'm doing my daily spiritual exercises from a sense of duty rather than love and not doing them regularly. Am I losing my faith, and how do I overcome this inner barrier?

It would be easy to beg off the question with "Don't worry; life will teach you better."

You are at one of life's many crossroads, which causes these feelings of doubt about your faith in ECK. But you can safely pass through this cycle by keeping your heart open to love.

Each life cycle has a growth and a fulfillment stage. We switch back and forth between them. The growth phase begins with a restless feeling that urges us into a new and greater opportunity, but fear holds us back. Finally, this need for growth outweighs the fear, so perhaps we risk a new job, enter a relationship, or return to school to improve our skills.

Each life cycle has a growth and a fulfillment stage. We switch back and forth between them.

What growth stage am I in?

What fulfillment stage am I in?

> Remember the goal: becoming a Co-worker with God. It includes seeing the good qualities in others as well as yourself.

How I am becoming a better Co-worker with God:

The growth phase then moves on to the fulfillment stage. Here, we master the new routines that come with change and plunge into the options of our unexplored life. All our attention is upon the challenges and rewards before us.

However, the old restlessness will return. It's nothing to worry about, though. It simply means that Soul is ready to embark upon a fresh adventure of growth and fulfillment.

The company of others on the path of ECK will help you move gracefully from the state of growth to fulfillment. This community will pass along the love and support of the Mahanta whenever your fears try to shut him out.

How do you overcome the inner barrier of doubt and fear?

Put your heart into every new venture, for the Mahanta has led you through a gateway of opportunity to help you reach a higher level of ability, love, and compassion.

You also need to address the habit of thinking so much about yourself. Remember the goal: becoming a Co-worker with God. It includes seeing the good qualities in others as well as yourself.

The ECK Rite of Passage

In ECKANKAR, the ECK Rite of Passage is one of the celebrations of life. What does this ceremony mean spiritually? How do you know when it is time to receive your Rite of Passage? Is there a recommended age range for it?

The ECK Rite of Passage is one of the celebrations of life. It celebrates a new stage in Soul's journey home to God. Namely, it marks a person's growth from childhood to the threshold of becoming an adult.

This ceremony is for a youth who wants to begin taking on more responsibility in life, as well as for making a personal commitment to the ECK teachings. And to accepting the Mahanta for one's spiritual guide.

Around age thirteen or so is generally the time for this celebration of life, but one may take it to perhaps age twenty-one.

A youth who wishes to celebrate the ECK Rite of Passage needs to know the basic teachings of ECK. You or your parents can get more information about that from any member of the ECK clergy.

You'll know when you're ready for it. Then ask.

The Future Depends on Free Will

In a talk you mentioned that we are fortunate to be able to meet together at Eckankar seminars so openly and that we may not always have this opportunity to do so in the future. What would cause such a change in our freedom?

The future depends mainly upon the choices that people make. It is called free will.

A crisis of large proportions does loom for the human race due to the population explosion. Yet there are other pressures too. Some of these are political or geological, but underneath, they merely reflect a widespread misunderstanding about karma.

The idea so many have today is that one can cheat, lie, or steal without any consequences. It's an illusion.

There's no such thing as a free lunch.

Negative thoughts, words, and deeds cause the spiritual forces to impose limits upon the exercise of such behavior. As the negative stream is shut down somewhat, to bring harmony into the picture again, the negative forces resist. They, in turn, impose natural or legal restrictions on all outer freedoms.

The future depends mainly upon the choices that people make. It is called free will.

Choices I am making and ways I exercise my free will:

How my choices affect the future:

It is very hard to keep your heart open today. The world sometimes spins a lot faster than we can run to keep up.

Ways I can keep my heart open:

The idea is of this order: If I can't have more candy, you can't either.

The changes to come may include a tighter economy, more terrorism, more government controls upon people's travel, finances, and communications. Not directly, of course. Things are done in much more subtle ways.

Changes will be "sold" to people as a direction good for them. In fact, they're good for no one in the end. But people will buy the clever spins, because they want to see them as in their own best interests.

It's the old lie of getting something for nothing.

So in reaction to this stream of negative human consciousness in action, the forces of nature will rebel. Look for lots of changes in the next ten to fifteen years.

To Keep Your Heart Open

I have trouble keeping my heart open sometimes. Do you have any advice for me?

You're not alone. It is very hard to keep your heart open today. The world sometimes spins a lot faster than we can run to keep up.

Especially in school.

Others go out of their way to hurt us and cause trouble. That pressure makes it harder to keep up with the work in class or to fit in with classmates. There are a lot of big questions about the future too. At this moment, you stand on the threshold between your childhood and adult years. A time of change, for sure.

Little things now will tend to blow up, or exaggerate, in importance. So these otherwise minor points will try to create monsters out of mice. More than ever, look to the Mahanta for love.

There is one last thing. To keep your heart open, do one small, unsung good deed every day in the Mahanta's name. I am always with you.

What Is a Miracle?

What is a miracle? How do we open our consciousness to them all the time?

A dictionary might say that a miracle is an event that shows God's intervention in a human crisis. That's only half of it.

What if a tragedy occurs and God did not step in to avert it? No miracle? Sometimes there is, but the miracle is in how the victim responds spiritually to the tragedy. No one is immune from troubles; this is earth, you must remember.

Often, one needs to look into a past life. Ask the Mahanta to show you in some way the reason for the distressful event—and your past deeds that brought on the present troubles. Things happen to let us grow.

Stay close to the Mahanta (do your spiritual exercises) and your consciousness will naturally open to see the miracles around you every day.

How Does the Mahanta Help?

How do you help people solve problems? If someone is feeling scared or hurt inside how do you help them, and how can you listen to so many?

Let's look at your first question. There are two ways to help people solve a problem: do it for them, or let them do most or all of it alone.

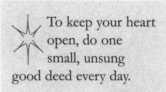

To keep your heart open, do one small, unsung good deed every day.

My spiritual insights:

To see the root of a problem is often all it takes to make a hurt fly away.

Look at a problem in your life. What does the root look like? Write or draw it here.

Which way do you think gives them more experience to care for themselves, to survive? And which way do you think builds the most confidence?

The second way, of course.

So the Mahanta, the Living ECK Master prefers to use the second method, unless there is a great, immediate need to help someone who is unable to do it alone. Either way, however, is an ECK miracle.

Second question . . .

The Master helps people overcome fear by showing them a way to solve or lessen their fearful situation. He gives hope. He grants ideas. He may send others to offer aid. He may also remove a threat with an out-and-out miracle.

And how to help those who hurt inside? He brings love. It comes to fill a heart in its darkest hour. Or, again, he may appear in a dream to show the karmic reason for the pain.

To see the root of a problem is often all it takes to make a hurt fly away.

Opening the Spiritual Eye

I'm a fourteen-year-old ECKist. Even though I do my spiritual exercises regularly I'm not having any experiences, like a dream or even just seeing a blue light. Can you please help me to have an experience? Also, my dad says he sees the ECK in everything. What does he mean?

May I encourage you to keep on with the Spiritual Exercises of ECK!

Remember how long it took to learn the skill of writing? Now you can dash off the alphabet without a second thought, as well as string combinations of letters together to form words and sentences.

The pattern of learning a spiritual skill requires much the same diligence. For a long time there may appear to be no progress at all, yet a foundation is in the making. By no means become frantic. The Mahanta waits until an individual gains a solid spiritual footing. Then he opens the Spiritual Eye.

That's what your dad is trying to explain when he says he sees the ECK (Divine Spirit) in everything.

The Master has opened his Spiritual Eye.

ECK has a thousand faces. Some see Its presence as some color of light, in dozens of possible shapes. Others, like your dad, see Its workings in everyday people, places, and situations.

ECK likewise has a thousand voices. Some hear It speak through any of dozens of possible voices: storms, birds, laughter, falling or moving water, rushing air, and even in the sounds of machinery.

Some perceive both the Light and Sound of God.

Give it time.

Let's see what can be done for you.

You Make Your Own Happiness

How can love be with me? This question is difficult for me because sometimes I feel sad. Happiness just seems to run out, and happiness is love.

Thank you for a very good question.

First, happiness isn't necessarily love. It's one of the things that comes from love. The Mahanta's love is always with you. That means he's with you in both happy and sad times, looking out for your best spiritual good.

Second, God is love, but not everything here is love. Remember, earth is a school. Soul (you) is here to learn how to become more like God's pure qualities of love. We learn most from our troubles, not always from the good times.

It helps to know this world for what it is—good and evil. The Mahanta's love helps you avoid many of the hard times and find the good.

Soul (you) is here to learn how to become more like God's pure qualities of love. We learn most from our troubles, not always from the good times.

What I am learning about love:

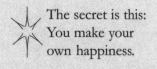

The secret is this: You make your own happiness.

There is only one of you in this world. But there are always a few people who think and feel as you do. Open your heart to them. Be their friend. Ignore the ones who are not like you.

The secret is this: You make your own happiness. And that begins with the company you keep.

Workbook:
Change and Growth

Key Insights
from This Chapter

- You make your own happiness.

- God's love is always with you.

- Change is an opportunity to grow spiritually.

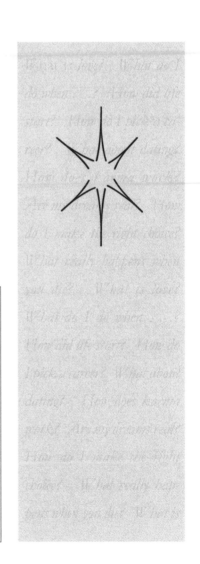

My key insights:

Spiritual Exercises to
Explore These Insights

1. For one day, practice doing everything, large or small, for God alone. Do everything for love, for God is love. That means do it with love, joy, and thoroughness. How does this change your outlook on life? What opportunities does it bring you?

   Record your insights here:

2. Write down three key turning points or changes in your life. Note how old you were, how you responded to each change, and what you learned from it:

	Turning point or change	My age	My response	What I learned
1				
2				
3				

Since change is an opportunity to grow spiritually, what change would you like to make in your life now?

3. Make your own book of wisdom about change.

    - Choose a blank book or notebook you like.

    - Create a colorful cover.

    - Research and write down quotes that inspire you about change and growth.

    - Talk to someone who has gone through a big change. Maybe they moved or started a new school or job. Ask them to tell you how they did it. Record in your book any of their tips and ideas that you like.

    - Use this book to help you with any changes you're facing in your life right now.

4. Divine Spirit is present all around us. To become more aware of how It is helping you through your changes, look for Its presence all day today. You may see Its workings in everyday people, places, and situations. Or you may see it as some color of light. Or you may hear It speak in the natural sounds of life.

    Record your observations and insights here:

5. You are Soul, here to learn spiritual lessons every day. What
   have you learned about yourself as you read this chapter?

The physical mind is limited like a little bucket. The inner experiences you have on the spiritual planes are like a vast ocean.

4

Past Lives, Dreams, and Soul Travel

How Dreams Can Help Us

How can our dreams help us?

Dreams are like a daily report card. They show how you are doing in your spiritual mission, even if you don't know you have one. Dreams tell how you are getting on in your relationship with God and life.

There is a spiritual side to every experience or event, no matter how large or small, and whether or not it occurs in everyday life or in a dream.

But—and this is a big *but*—few people have the spiritual eyes to see.

Most people are in a daze but don't know it. They have hardly any idea about their life in the higher spiritual worlds while their body lies asleep at day's end.

Dreams are like a daily report card. But few people have the spiritual eyes to see.

Each person is Soul, capable of being fully aware twenty-four hours a day. The lessons of life come to us every minute, on every level.

What I am aware of right now as Soul:

Dreams Are Real

Are the people and places in my dreams real? Are other people having the same dream as I am?

A dream is a real experience. As Soul—the spiritual being you are as a divine spark of God—you can (and do) have hundreds of experiences going on side by side at different levels. So does everyone else.

Here is a way to understand the variety of inner experiences: it's as if Soul experiences what hundreds of people in a town do on a certain day. The mind, meanwhile, can recall only a few experiences at a time.

You may remember a certain inner experience with someone on the inner planes because of its spiritual importance for you. However, the other person will likely remember a completely different experience, because your needs are different.

In comparison to Soul, our mind holds only a few memories at a time. We remember those that mean the most to us spiritually.

Only rarely do the spiritual needs of two people exactly coincide. When they do, both dreamers will remember the same dream. However, their different levels of consciousness will give each a special view of what actually happened in the dream state.

How to Learn from Your Dreams

What does the dream state represent that the waking state does not?

There is no difference in my mind. Each person is Soul, capable of being fully aware twenty-four hours a day. The lessons of life come to us every minute, on every level. However, few people today pay much mind to the power of Soul and Its being. The average person goes through life with only the barest sense of his or her true identity as Soul, a spark of God.

Becoming Aware of Dreams

Why can't I be aware of all my dreams? Why do I forget them after I awaken in the morning? How can I remember my dreams better?

There can be any number of reasons. The physical mind is limited, like a little bucket. The inner experiences you have on all the spiritual planes are like a vast ocean. It is useless trying to pour the ocean into the mind's little bucket.

Soul is running several bodies at the same time on other planes. Its scope of action is much greater than the recall ability of the dreamer's mind.

Sometimes the mind wants to protect you because the dream would shock you. It's a different world with different rules. You wake up here, and right away this world crowds in on you. And you say, "I've got to get up, go to school or work."

Some people naturally enjoy vivid recollections of their dream state, but those who don't can develop the skill.

You can set a dream in your mind as you wake up by repeating the points of it, then talking about it out loud or writing it down as soon as you get up.

It is also possible to develop a sharper recall of the dream state by keeping a notebook by the bed, with pen and light at hand. Make a resolution to wake—even in the middle of the night—to record any memory of the dream state, no matter how trivial it seems.

Clues about Who You Are

What can dreams tell us about ourselves?

Dreams hint at truth. I say *hint* instead of *tell* for a reason: Most people don't actually want to know the

Make a resolution to wake—even in the middle of the night—to record any memory of the dream state, no matter how trivial it seems.

A dream I remember:

As with all things of a divine nature, accept each dream as a spiritual gift. Wonder about it.

What I think this dream could mean:

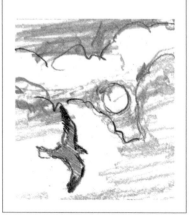

truth. The truth hurts. Dreams can tell us when we're unkind, unfair, vengeful, selfish, and other unpleasant facts that we need to work on spiritually. But truth makes most people uncomfortable, so they shut it out and forget their dreams.

I've tried many dream systems and have kept a record of my own inner travels for years. Of all the systems, the dream methods of Eckankar are the golden thread that have been of the most use to me for spiritual growth.

Messages in Dreams

Sometimes I have trouble finding the lesson or message in my dreams. Some of them seem just too wacky to even have one! Does each dream have a spiritual meaning or lesson involved? Or are some just purely creations of my imagination?

Every experience, waking or dream, has a lesson or message to impart to us. But let the meanings of your inner and outer experiences come naturally. In other words, if the lesson or message isn't clear, don't force it.

Soul, the spiritual self that you are, will send another dream again in some other way until your human self can easily grasp the meaning.

In Eckankar, dream study works on all levels. As with all things of a divine nature, accept each dream as a spiritual gift. Wonder about it. Roll it gently around in your mind to see whether loving patience on your part will reveal its significance.

This approach is the reason the Eckankar spiritual studies are called the Easy Way.

One other point.

Dream experiences are real experiences from another time, place, or dimension. Some of them are from past lives, which you'd expect to be straight-forward. Yet here's where the mind—or what you called "just purely creations of my imagination?"—comes in.

The dream censor is a function, or part, of the mind. For purely karmic reasons it may decide that a certain past life would be too much of a shock to you. You might break off a relationship. Yet that relation-ship in the present time may be necessary to bring an important insight to you.

So the dream censor tones down dreams. It lets a dreamer go ahead with life and so profit from past-life experiences.

As Soul, You Can Be Several Places at the Same Time

I was having a dream about one thing, and some other dream jumped in and interrupted. In fact, about five different dreams did that. I was dreaming about being in a pasture and then some ninjas jumped out and attacked me. What does this mean, if anything? Why do dreams do that?

Dreams do not really jump in on each other at all. What happens is that you, in the Soul body, are jump-ing from one inner experience to another.

Soul can be in several different places at the same time. This is not unusual, because Soul runs at least one body on each of the lower planes, and sometimes more. What you see as skipping from one dream to another is like switching TV channels to see what programs are on. Such skipping about gets old, so we usually settle down to watch whatever interests us the most, like your dream of the ninjas.

Your experience with the ninjas in that dream world was real. When we watch violence on TV, it

Dream experiences are real experiences from another time, place, or dimension.

How a dream has helped me in my life:

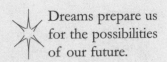
Dreams prepare us for the possibilities of our future.

Use this space for your journal:

means we are in agreement with it inwardly. This opens us to nightmares. It's better to watch happier programs or read uplifting books, if we want more restful dreams.

Dreams Prepare Us for the Future

In a recent dream I saw a situation which I understood to be a possibility in my future. Although I would eventually welcome it, I know that I am not ready for such a big step now. So I wonder why this would reveal itself to me at this time.

Dreams prepare us for the possibilities of our future. A young girl may dream of becoming a wife years before she's ready for such a role. Later, her ideas may swing away from her youthful dreams of marriage, and new ones replace them.

But when the time comes for marriage, she is ready. She is ready to step into the role of a marriage partner with more love and confidence than she would have had as a girl. This is so because of her dreams.

Our dreams simply prepare us for many future possibilities. We can then decide which future path we want to go for.

What Is Illusion, What Is Truth?

Are the friends and family members I meet in my dreams actually sharing the experience? Is it as real for them as it is for me (though they may not remember)? Or are they only present as mock-ups in my mind?

You may all have the same dream experience. Yet there are times when your mind will create a fantasy world, like a dramatist who moves characters around in a play. How do you tell the difference? What is illusion; what is truth?

The key is the Spiritual Exercises of ECK. They help you sort out the real experiences from the false ones.

Some people tell other people about their dreams in order to control others. For example, a man tells a woman about his dream where she agreed to marry him. It's a choke hold. His intentions should stand on their own merits. That means he should simply say he loves her. Then it's up to her to decide whether the relationship holds anything for her without the pressure of trying to live up to his dream.

As I've said before—the inner is for the inner; the outer is for the outer.

From Dreaming to Soul Travel

I used to have an experience that I wish you would explain. Whenever I was waking up from sleep, I would feel as though I were falling from a great height and as if I were out of my body. I was never afraid because I felt familiar with the vibrations of those heights. What was most interesting was the beautiful music I always heard. Often I heard madrigals, with mostly female voices.

When you were waking up, Soul was coming back to the body from the higher planes. This gave you the feeling of falling from a great height and was a Soul Travel experience.

Hearing the madrigal indicates Soul Travel on the Mental Plane, since this form of song particularly develops the Mental body. The madrigal is another expression of the Sound Current there in addition to the sound of running water.

This experience shows you are being prepared for the high spiritual planes in this lifetime.

> The key is the Spiritual Exercises of ECK. They help you sort out the real experiences from the false ones.

Try a spiritual exercise. What did you experience?

To avoid making karma, while either awake or asleep, sing the word *HU.* You can do this quietly within yourself or out loud. It's an ancient name for God.

When I sing HU quietly or out loud, I notice:

Karma in the Dream State

Can we create karma in our dreams? If so, how? And how can we avoid it?

Yes, people can create karma in the dream state. Yet most are unaware that they do so, even as they are unaware of karma they make every day.

Each of us is like a power station. We generate energy all the time, energy that can either build or destroy. If we let unworthy thoughts or desires leave our power station, they pollute everything around us. That is bad karma. Our mind is like a machine, able to issue contaminants around the clock. Our thoughts even run on automatic at night, when we may unconsciously try to control others or harm them in the dream state.

The problem is a lack of spiritual self-discipline.

To avoid making karma, while either awake or asleep, sing the word *HU.* You can do this quietly within yourself or out loud. It's an ancient name for God. Sing it when you are angry, frightened, or alone. HU calms and restores, because it sets your thoughts upon the highest spiritual ideal. People from any walk of life can sing HU for spiritual upliftment.

Déjà Vu

I would like to know the meaning of déjà vu. *Recently, I have quite often been struck by pictures or remembrances of things I have already seen or lived. Could it be that I dreamed my entire life before?*

Déjà vu is a strong feeling of already having experienced something before.

Life is a dream from beginning to end. Some people, like you, have the unusual ability of bringing the memory of a dream into the present moment.

That is the reason so many things are already familiar to you. It is a special ability, but remember that other people have their special gifts too. That's why this world is such an interesting place to live.

You Have Inner Bodies

Sometimes when I am dreaming, I wake up to find I am still dreaming. And I wake up again to find myself waking up in yet another dream. I have counted as many as fifteen or twenty of these awakenings before I am awake on the outer. What is this experience?

This is an excellent sign of your spiritual growth.

As Soul, you can run a number of bodies at one time. For instance, one of the inner worlds, the Astral Plane, has about 150 distinct levels, or heavens, in it; Soul may materialize a body in any number of those subplanes. The Causal Plane, the place where memories and karmic patterns are stored, is described as having many more levels than that. Therefore, in the Soul body, you may actually run twenty or more bodies at once in the other worlds.

During the process of waking up, Soul is returning from these far places, and you may momentarily remember each of your inner bodies in turn. By the time you wake up here, your attention is completely nested in your physical body again for everyday life at school, work, or home.

The multiple awakenings show your developing growth in the worlds of God.

As Soul, you can run a number of bodies at one time. During the process of waking up, Soul is returning from these far places, and you may momentarily remember each of your inner bodies in turn.

Have you ever been aware of dreams within dreams? Write about or draw one here:

You can begin exploring your interests in these fields of knowledge through dreams or Soul Travel.

Choose something you're interested in and explore it in a dream or Soul Travel. What did you learn?

Meeting Your Past in Dreams

In my dreams, I am often with friends from the past whom I no longer see in the physical. These people had a big influence in my life at one time, but why are they in my dreams so often today?

Your question deals with the very broad sweep of reincarnation. The family you live with today is only a small part of the extended family from your past.

Each person's past link with other people in this life is more like being a member of a far-flung clan, which goes well beyond the close members of today's family. So in this life, other members of your extended family come as schoolmates, friends of childhood, teachers, and the like.

They remain in your dreams because they are a very real part of you. For this lifetime, though, they have chosen a different mission and lifestyle, so you go along your separate paths.

But your inner bond spans time.

All Animals Dream

I would like to know if animals such as lions, cows, and dogs have Soul Travel experiences.

Some animals do. They're the same as people, in that animals have many different levels of consciousness.

Like us, all animals dream. Some remember, many don't. Specially gifted ones, like spiritually advanced people, do Soul Travel. In time, scientific research will be able to expand its knowledge of what happens when people and animals sleep.

You can begin exploring your interests in these fields of knowledge through dreams or Soul Travel. Eventually, science will catch up to the knowledge of those who already can explore the spiritual states of living beings—human or animal—by Soul Travel.

Who Is the Dream Master?

In my dream, I walked up into some hills, and it seemed like the Fourth of July. Thousands of people were sitting in the hills looking into the sky as if expecting fireworks. The sky was light blue and free of clouds.

I walked past the crowds until I was alone again and looked at the hills in the distance. They were like hard-packed sand dunes without vegetation. Suddenly, a flash of red went by and stopped long enough for me to recognize it before disappearing. It was me. That made me feel really odd. Looking out over the ridge of hills, I saw that they had undergone a drastic change. They were much lumpier, and a huge boulder with green vines all over it had been raised ten feet into the air.

The dream felt very real. I had just gone through a doorway and was expecting a member of an ancient American race that I had just read about in a Louis L'Amour novel. But I woke up before he arrived.

This is what your dream means: Your walk up into the hills indicates that in the dream you were moving into a higher state of consciousness.

The Fourth of July is Independence Day. The Mahanta, who is also the Dream Master, used this image to evoke in you the ideal of spiritual freedom, which you can achieve in this lifetime if you set your heart upon it.

The thousands of people are your collective awareness—i.e., the sum total of your thoughts and hopes. You are awaiting the ecstasy of spiritual freedom. The blue sky signifies the Blue Light of the Mahanta, the Inner Master, which students of Eckankar often see in their dreams and spiritual exercises. When you leave the crowds, it means you leave behind your worries and come to rest in Soul, the center of your being.

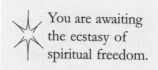

You are awaiting the ecstasy of spiritual freedom.

What spiritual freedom means to me:

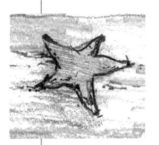

This dream shows how the Dream Master may shape your dream to help you better understand yourself.

Ask the Dream Master to teach you something new about yourself. What did you find out?

You are now in the Soul body and look back on the hills, which are nothing more than events in your daily life. From the lofty vantage point of Soul, your outer life seems to be a spiritual wasteland, especially when you let anger (the "flash of red") flare up.

The image of the boulder is used in a double sense here. First, Soul studies the ridge of hills to see what harm anger might do, and It perceives a "much lumpier" life. Anger makes mountains out of mole-hills, or in this case, a huge boulder is raised ten feet into the air.

Second, green vines clinging to the face of the boulder show the power of envy or jealousy to under-mine a relationship. Have you heard the phrase "green with envy"? The roots of the vines can, in time, shatter the greatest boulder, just as envy and jealousy can destroy the closest relationship, even one that seems "solid as a rock."

The member of an ancient Ameri-can race whom you were expecting was the Mahanta, the Living ECK Master.

This dream gives a most exacting look at yourself. It shows how the Dream Master may shape your dream to help you better understand yourself.

Study Your Dreams

People in my dreams never act the way they do in real life. Why? Am I really with that person on the inner, or not? When I dream of other people, is it about them or what they represent to me? How can I distin-guish between the two? How do I find a balance be-tween the dream world and my physical life? If I have a disturbing dream about someone, how can I under-stand the spiritual gift and then let it go?

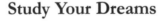

You really are with that person on the inner. But a couple of things come into play.

First, you may not remember the inner experience exactly as it happened. The dream censor is responsible for that. He represents the social part of the Kal, the negative force. His reason is that you're not ready to handle the truth—which may be true. So your recall is clouded. That's illusion. It protects you from emotional shocks.

Second, your distorted recall of the dream will *represent* a hidden truth, instead of giving the actual truth face-to-face. So you must decipher it by asking the Mahanta for help in understanding. Ask him for help during contemplation.

Every well-balanced person finds a balance between the dream world and the physical life. Remember, the physical laws are for the physical world, while laws of the dream world are for the dream world. Keep them separate. Unless you do, you're likely to blunder into some terrible mistakes.

For example, let's say someone in your dream expresses ardent love for you. You take that for his true feelings in the physical world. He may not be aware of them yet and will consider your sudden friendliness pushy. He'll back right off, afraid of you. Actually he's afraid of something he wasn't prepared for—your love.

In this case, play it cool. Feel out the situation a little at a time. Test the waters. Also be ready to accept the fact that this relationship will never develop. Here again, the realities of the dream world may not be suitable for the physical world.

Study your dreams. You'll learn what your dreams mean to your physical life with the Mahanta's help. You keep in touch with him by doing the Spiritual Exercises of ECK. Some are given at the end of this chapter.

> Remember, the physical laws are for the physical world, while laws of the dream world are for the dream world. Keep them separate.

What do my dreams mean to my physical life?

Apply the principle of the waking dream to your dream world. The people you meet there are Souls, just like you.

My spiritual insights:

Are the Dream Worlds Real?

How can I tell whether the people I meet in the dream state are other Souls or just symbolic parts of myself?

The dream worlds and its people are real. It is only our recall and understanding of it that are incomplete. Our link with the inner worlds is usually through dreams, but illusion can make our memory of inner events faulty.

What about the dream people who appear to be just symbolic parts of ourselves? Let's start with the waking dream. The Mahanta, the Inner Master, uses it to give someone a spiritual insight from an experience in his daily life. The Master draws on the individual's experiences with real people and real events to point out some personal truth.

Apply the principle of the waking dream to your dream world. The people you meet there are Souls, just like you. However, the Mahanta can turn your experiences with them into an open window of understanding, to unlock your desires, needs, and goals.

Admittedly, Eckankar is nearly alone in treating the dream world as real. More paths and teachings will someday reach the same understanding, but only after their people travel consciously in the other worlds as many members of Eckankar do.

The Real Thing

What is the difference between Soul Travel and dream travel?

It's like watching a video of someone playing in a warm, sunny pool of water or swimming in that pool yourself.

The video shows the sun upon the waters. But if you are in the pool itself, you feel the sunbeams warm your arms and body. The video shows someone else splashing, but in real life you feel the soft kiss of droplets wash over your face and hair.

Do you see? It's like that.

Yet a Soul Travel experience is more real than even a splash in the pool. Soul Travel makes every color around you, every touch, every scent of a flower, every birdsong or tinkling bell seem as if their very atoms have taken on a life of their own.

You feel as if life itself were hugging and kissing you. And blessing you.

Hard as one tries, it's beyond the art of human language to tell the whole story about Soul Travel. But a dream is just a dream. It's like something happening to us at arm's length.

Soul Travel is the real thing.

The reason Soul Travel is so full of life is that in the Soul body we rise in consciousness. We are closer to the full awareness of ECK, the Divine Spirit.

Only Fear Stops Us from Soul Travel

When fear stops me from continuing a Soul Travel experience, can anything help me overcome that fear?

First of all, I'm glad to see you using the word *continuing*. It means that you have at least had a little experience with Soul Travel.

You are right, it is only fear that stops us from having any progress with Soul Travel. What happens when you love someone or something with your whole heart? Right, fear is pushed out of your mind!

Therefore, can you go into contemplation by putting a thought into your heart about something you did once that made you happier than you've ever been before?

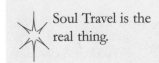

Soul Travel is the real thing.

What Soul Travel means to me:

Keep on imagining that you do Soul Travel, and one day you will suddenly do it.

Imagine you can Soul Travel. What happened?

Then take with you the thought: "I love God with all that is within me." This takes practice, of course.

I hope that this will help you get over your fear. It is quite a natural thing, but you will see it growing less powerful as you keep on with the spiritual exercises.

Imagination and Soul Travel

I've heard that we should use our imagination to Soul Travel, but can we use too much imagination? Sometimes I'll have an experience and not be sure whether I've made it up or what.

To imagine Soul Travel is the first thing one must do before actually getting out of the body.

A girl who plays second base for the baseball team in town is called a "natural." But she works hard at her fielding and hitting. Her brothers are all good ball players, and in her mind she imagines herself every bit as good as they are. And so she *is* good, not only because of her imagination, but mainly because she practices harder than the other girls on the team.

Keep on imagining that you do Soul Travel, and one day you will suddenly do it. You will have no more doubt about the difference between imagination and Soul Travel. Wait and see!

Golden Wisdom Temples and ECK Masters

One night I had a beautiful dream. I went with Wah Z, the Inner Master, to a place where there was a huge castle and a blue sun. ECK Master Rebazar Tarzs came flying out of the sun and landed in front of us. Then he and Wah Z and I went into the castle. Inside I saw many ECK Masters and heard a beautiful flute playing. I wondered where it was coming from. Then I saw a blue light and followed it until I came to a door where bright light shone around the edges. I opened the door and saw ECK Master Yaubl Sacabi playing the flute. Where was I?

I'm glad you remembered your visit to the place of the huge castle and blue sun. It is on the Mental Plane. Rebazar Tarzs coming out of the sun meant out of the heart of Sugmad (God). The castle is actually one of the Golden Wisdom Temples. This is the reason why you saw all the ECK Masters there. They come to teach Souls to hear and see the Sound and Light of God.

Some people think that Paul Twitchell, the founder of Eckankar, and I made up the idea about real ECK Masters like Rebazar Tarzs, Yaubl Sacabi, and the rest. These people still have to learn how to love the Holy Spirit above all things, the way you do. Otherwise the ECK Masters cannot take them into the beautiful worlds of ECK.

Healing Your Past Lives in Dreams

Why do we have bad dreams?

A good dream is one that helps you grow stronger, wiser, and more full of love.

So what are bad dreams for?

Children often have nightmares until the age of six or eight, and sometimes longer. Grown-ups do too, though not so often as a rule. But why bad dreams for good people?

A bad dream is generally a memory of a past life. It may include experiences of mistreatment, suffering, and even death. Some of us even have dreams of being born, which can give a feeling of suffocation. These experiences are part of everyone. Children still remember bits and pieces of past lives, and these bad dreams are a part of them.

Bad dreams are old fears.

A bad dream is generally a memory of a past life. Bad dreams are old fears.

Write down a bad dream. How is it a past-life memory or an old fear?

Your interest in that period of history is due to your many past lives there.

Some interests I have:

Having a bad dream is like airing out a musty room in spring. You need to face that old fear until it loses its grip, for only then can you be free to live this life to its fullest.

So good and bad dreams both hold spiritual lessons.

Attractions from Past Lives

I haven't been having any dreams that I can remember for the past month. This is unusual for me; I usually have dreams all the time. Is it karma? I would like to know, if possible, because I learn from my dreams.

Another thing I would like to know is are there knights on the inner planes? I am attracted to medieval wars and battles.

In answer to your first question: By the time you read this, you will have started to dream again. There are times when Soul shifts gears; this is when we don't always remember our dreams. But it is a passing thing.

About your attraction to knights and medieval wars and battles: Your interest in that period of history is due to your many past lives there. It was a time of great adventure, chivalry, and heroics. The forces of darkness and light were in a hotly contested battle for centuries, and you played a part in those unsettled, but interesting, times.

History can teach us much about how mankind's unlearned lessons repeat themselves. This allows us to use our knowledge to avoid unnecessary problems, because we can sidestep a lot of them.

People make history. You might enjoy the historical novels of Mary Stewart about Merlin that bring to life the times of King Arthur at the beginning of the Middle Ages: *The Crystal Cave, The Hollow Hills, The*

Last Enchantment, and *The Wicked Day.* You'll find many spiritual insights in her books, for she is adept at looking at past-life records on the Causal Plane. The books are in the library.

Mary Stewart's novels may be too hard for you to read yet, because they are for adults. If so, ask your librarian if she has other books about King Arthur that you might like to read.

Awakening Your Past-Life Memories

I would like to see my past lives. How do I go about this?

It is easiest to trace past lives through a study of your dreams.

To awaken such past-life dreams, make a note of things you greatly like or dislike. Do that also with people. Then watch your dreams. Also note if a certain country or century attracts you. There is a reason.

When we practice the Spiritual Exercises of ECK faithfully, the Inner Master will open us up to those things that are important to see concerning past lives. Most of them need not concern us. No matter what we were in the past during any other life, we are spiritually greater today.

The wealth and position we enjoyed in past lives mean nothing unless we know how to lift ourselves from materialism into the higher worlds. This does not mean to shun the good things of this life—family, home, wealth. God loves the rich man as much as the poor. We get no special benefits if we fall for the negative tricks of asceticism or unusual austerities.

We live the spiritual life beginning where we are today. We look to see the hand of Divine Spirit guiding us toward the greater consciousness, which leads us to becoming a more direct vehicle for Spirit.

It is easiest to trace past lives through a study of your dreams.

To awaken such past-life dreams, make a note of things you greatly like or dislike.

Things I like:

Things I dislike:

> Grace and respect are two signs of a mature spiritual individual, whatever his religion or beliefs.

How are you developing grace and respect in your life?

The Truth about Reincarnation

People reincarnate to resolve karma created in past lifetimes. But, observing world events, it seems people are creating more karma for themselves. Will people learn to work together while resolving their karma? If we take responsibility for our actions, then when will our karma be finished so reincarnation is no longer necessary?

The whole process of refining Souls through resolving karma made in past lives is a slow, careful one. The mills of karma grind slowly, but exceedingly fine.

Yes, people are very busy every day creating new karma for themselves. The reason is they overreact to every slight. They show a lack of respect first for themselves, then for others. They need still to develop the quality of grace. Grace and respect are two signs of a mature spiritual individual, whatever his religion or beliefs.

Karma works itself off by levels, through the hard experiences of life. The University of Hard Knocks. A Soul that completes a certain level of purification then graduates to a higher level of choice, experience, and service.

You'll find that many leaders in politics belong to the school of adolescent Souls. It explains their shortsighted and irresponsible behavior as the supposed representatives of their electorate. But they too will someday move above their own limitations.

For a better understanding about the workings of karma, read Dr. Michael Newton's book *Journey of Souls* (Llewellyn Publications, St. Paul, Minnesota). The knowledge in it should give you a greater degree of contentment.

What Eckankar Can Offer You

I had a dream in which I was walking down a sidewalk with a friend at 9:00 p.m. I looked up in the sky and saw the moon, which looked huge. Beside the moon was a big planet with a ring around it. Everyone else in the dream seemed to take no notice but carried on as if it were just an ordinary day. I was excited and wanted to know why the moon and planet were there. Can you please explain to me what this dream means?

Yours is a spiritual dream. The sidewalk is the path of Eckankar. Since it's your dream and your path, the lessons will be yours—not your friend's. Evening means the end of Soul's karmic day: this life is your gateway to spiritual freedom. Looking up into the sky indicates your high spiritual vision. The huge moon is the promise of a brighter life in ECK, here and now.

The big planet with the ring is a symbol for the great worlds of God beyond our own. You alone, of all the others in the dream, were thrilled at the sight of the moon and planet because of your appreciation for spiritual things. Overall, the dream means you may go with the Mahanta to the spiritual worlds of ECK.

If you would like to see them, say at bedtime, "Wah Z (my spiritual name), show me the wonder of God's creation."

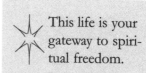
This life is your gateway to spiritual freedom.

Write a spiritual dream you've had:

Workbook:
Past Lives, Dreams, and Soul Travel

Key Insights
from This Chapter

- Your dreams are real experiences.

- Soul Travel is moving in consciousness in your inner worlds.

- You, as Soul, have had many past lives.

My key insights:

Spiritual Exercises to Explore These Insights

1. Think of a significant dream you have had. Make a note of it.
    For one week, keep a record of your dreams. Are there any
    images, symbols, or feelings that reappear? What do they mean
    to you? Ask the Dream Master to help you understand what
    they mean.

    Write down what you get:

Image, symbol, or feeling   **Possible meaning**

_____   _____

_____   _____

_____   _____

_____   _____

_____   _____

_____   _____

_____   _____

_____   _____

_____   _____

_____   _____

_____   _____

2. At bedtime, fill your heart with love and ask the Mahanta, the Inner Master, to show you what Soul Travel is like. When you wake, write what you remember here:

3. Dreams can open the window of understanding. Tonight, use
   your dreams to get insight into a problem or challenge you may
   have in your life. Before bed, write it out on a piece of paper.
   Phrase it as a question you are asking someone that you trust.
   Then put the piece of paper under your pillow. In the morning,
   write or draw a picture in the space below, describing what you
   dreamed about (even if it seems like it is different than what
   you asked about).

4. After reviewing this dream information, ask the Mahanta inwardly for three positive actions you can take to solve the problem. Write your ideas here:

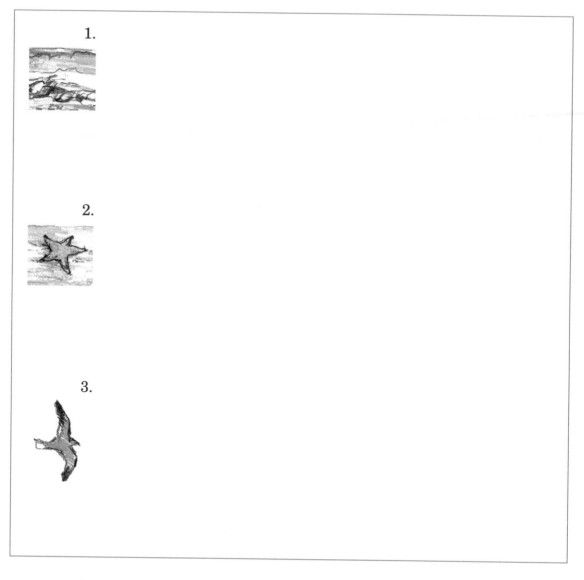

1.

2.

3.

Repeat this exercise if you feel you need more insights.

5. Your interests and talents often come from your many past lives. Make a list of places or things you're interested in, or used to be when you were younger, which could come from past lives:

<table>
<tr><th>Places</th><th>Things</th></tr>
<tr><td>_____</td><td>_____</td></tr>
<tr><td>_____</td><td>_____</td></tr>
<tr><td>_____</td><td>_____</td></tr>
<tr><td>_____</td><td>_____</td></tr>
<tr><td>_____</td><td>_____</td></tr>
<tr><td>_____</td><td>_____</td></tr>
</table>

Soul has no beginning or ending. What are these interests and talents teaching you about yourself, as Soul, in your life today?

6. You are Soul, here to learn spiritual lessons every day. What have you learned about yourself as you read this chapter?

Competition is all right as long as a person develops and follows a code of fair play.

5

SPIRITUAL CHOICES

How Do You Make Choices?

In making choices, how can someone tell whether he is being guided by divine love or by the mind?

You can't ever be sure.

Why?

The mind has a power to make you believe you are always right. That's why a headstrong person acts so smart. He thinks he's always right, though he's often wrong.

So, then, what is the good of ECK?

If guided by divine love, we are more likely to change our minds when new information comes along. We're quicker to admit that an earlier decision based on sketchy information needs to change. Those under the guidance of the ECK, or Holy Spirit, are always alert.

Identify Your Purpose

How do I know what my purpose in this lifetime is?

Those under the guidance of the ECK, or Holy Spirit, are always alert.

115

You know your *general* purpose is to become a Co-worker with God. So how do you identify your *personal* goal?

A personal goal I have now is:

You know your *general* purpose is to become a Co-worker with God. So how do you identify your *personal* goal?

Let's say you're a writer planning to write a novel. It is the story of your life. You may drive your story by one of two approaches: by plot or character. Let me explain.

If you plan your life by plot (a master plan), the rest of your life will reflect your spiritual unfoldment at the time of planning. This is a narrow approach. You will reject any experience outside the original plan. It leaves no room for freedom.

A plot-driven story has every detail planned. However, it creates a character (you) whose understanding of life is thin, like a piece of cardboard. Such a person is stiff, afraid of people's opinions, and failure crushes him easily. He or she weighs every act by an outside authority, such as what people might think.

On the other hand, a character-driven story is like a life guided by the Sound and Light of God. Yes, we do plan. However, in this approach, we recognize the superiority of Soul over any plan. Therefore, if the Holy Spirit, the ECK, brings a new direction into our life, which falls outside our original master plan, we contemplate upon it. We are willing to change our direction.

This character-driven approach to living is fresh. It can accept spontaneity. We see the ECK's guidance as a moment-to-moment reality. It is a better guide than our mind, which creates the plot-driven life.

So how do you learn your purpose?

The Mahanta will bring you many right seasons for spiritual growth. Contemplate upon them. Only at the end of your life will you be certain of what your personal goal was and if you have achieved it.

In the meantime, plan for a full, rich life of love and service to God and others.

Heart or Head?

Our minds play such an important role in our lives and they have a place, but in serious situations how do you know when to listen to your heart instead of just the facts and information inside your head? How do you know when your heart is speaking (and not just fear or sympathy)?

You've hit upon the whole problem of living. When does one listen to the heart or the head?

If it's any consolation to you, that's the great mystery which ages upon ages of people have struggled to understand. In a pure sense the two camps, which include everyone, are the head and the heart people. But no one's all one or the other.

From what I've seen, those who are mostly head, or mind, people have a harder time in trying to deal with the hard questions of life.

Some of these hard questions include: What is love? Does God really exist? Is there life after death? In each case a mind person wants proof. Until it comes he takes the position: Since I don't know the answer, no one else can either.

Even more, a mind person is likely to go out of his way to destroy the beliefs of others. So a mind person is apt to be rigid and unforgiving in regard to the beliefs of others. A mind person is basically of a juvenile mind. He's still young in spiritual experience.

The heart person takes what life has to offer and is grateful for its blessings. Life is relatively simple for him. (Oddly, a mind person probably considers a heart person a simpleminded fool.)

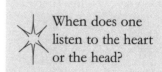

When does one listen to the heart or the head?

I listen to my heart when:

I listen to my head when:

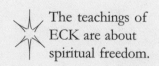

The teachings of ECK are about spiritual freedom.

Try looking at a problem from the top. What do you see?

But no matter. A heart person tends toward love, patience, and tolerance. He is like sunshine to others.

Head person: When faced with a complicated knot in a rope, he tries to unravel each strand.

Heart person: Like Alexander the Great, he simply cuts the rope and conquers all. Because he's rich in spiritual experience, he quickly gets to the heart of things.

Social Issues

At Eckankar seminars, you have talked about abortion, AIDS, and homosexuality. I find these topics very important today, especially with the youth over eighteen. Why aren't these issues formally addressed in workshops at seminars?

They are social issues. The main purpose of the ECK teachings is to help people find their way back home to God, no matter what their circumstances in life.

People have all sorts of problems in life, simply because that is the way of things on earth. There are those who have to deal with heart disease, cancer, mental and emotional problems, old age, deafness, war in their homeland, crime on the streets, and even the effects of accidents.

The teachings of ECK are about spiritual freedom. The main focus in Eckankar is not on relationships, an abused childhood, or any of the other social conditions that result from karma that people bring from the past. We look at these problems from the top. How can people gain in spiritual freedom and not do in the future more of what has brought on their problems of today?

Yes, we must deal with the issues of daily life. However, we also must watch our emotions and not let them trap us into tunnel vision.

This would only bring on more lifetimes in spiritual darkness.

AIDS

What is the truth about the phenomenon of AIDS, and how can we protect ourselves from it?

AIDS is just another of the serious illnesses that periodically sweep the earth.

In the fourteenth century, for example, the Black Death, or bubonic plague, killed from a quarter to a third of Europe's population in three years. Standards of hygiene were much lower than today. Bubonic plague was transmitted by the fleas on black rats. The waste of its victims gave others pneumonic plague. Europe had no defense against either, because of its low consciousness about hygiene.

The problem with AIDS again is a matter of awareness. Health agencies have made available much information of how to be careful with sexual intimacy. It means taking the trouble to first find out the state of your partner's health and other considerations.

Effect of Our Musical Choices

Do certain types of music affect people negatively? If so, how?

Let's say this: The music you like tells a lot about you. Some music is uplifting, while other music is not. Certain music is harsh, yet that does not mean it is not music. Take, for example, the music of the Chinese, Japanese, or Indian people. It may hurt the ears of many people in the West, as does bagpipe music. Yet it is the choice of millions. So what is negative music?

Usually, it is music not to our liking.

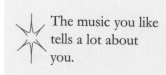

The music you like tells a lot about you.

The kind of music I like is:

What it says about me:

> A problem arises when one gets so caught up in the passion of doing something that it begins to take over his life.

My spiritual insights:

Music can break up thought forms in a society. For example, look at the music of Elvis Presley and the Beatles. At first, the media made fun of it. That soon changed.

Teens' music is sure to offend parents, and vice versa. Music, like anything else, becomes very negative when we try to push our tastes off on others—like blaring our music in public. A spiritual person has a high regard for the rights of others.

And yes, many people do serious harm to their ears by playing music too loudly through headsets. That is a very negative side of music—though of volume and not of kind.

TV, Computer, Movies, and Video Games

What effect does playing video and computer games, or watching TV and movies have on us? Is there any karma involved? Are there ways to protect oneself yet still play or watch them?

All activity involves karma—good or bad.

That said, there seems no way to escape it. But, yes, there is. That is, to do everything in the name of the Mahanta.

Easy?

Actually, no. A problem arises when one gets so caught up in the passion of doing something that it begins to take over his life. He'll always come up with a good reason why a passion out of control is a necessary activity. In short, he's kidding himself.

That's the nature of illusion. It clouds people's minds.

In the heyday of comic books, in the 1940s and 1950s, alarmists railed against them for ruining the young. Those youths are sixty and seventy today. The only thing that seems to ruin them is hard living and old age.

Before comics the day's evil was penny novels.
Then, radio adventure serials.
Next, TV.
Now, computer and video games.
So the more things change, the more they stay the same.

What, then, does one do? Walk the middle path, being aware to not stray from it too far to the left or right. Observe how much of your time does computing require? Is there time to keep up with (noncomputer) friends, get out among people, keep fit with exercise?

Computers like to take over. Don't let them. There's too much to do and learn outside of a computer's case. Listen to the Mahanta, your spiritual guide. Do your spiritual exercises.

Ouija Boards

My brothers and I got a Ouija board, and I was just wondering, are Ouija boards safe? Some people say it attracts evil spirits and other bad things.

A Ouija board is a dangerous "toy."

Yes, it does attract evil spirits, who, at best, play harmless tricks on people. At worst, they attack the Soul whose body it is, drive out that Soul, then take over the body. If the owner Soul is too strong to drive out completely, the evil spirits will try to settle for a chunk of body and mind space.

Possession by evil spirits accounts for people's sudden change in personality.

Then there's the split personality. That's when one or more evil spirits and the owner Soul take turns in the driver's seat, like driving a car. Such a person is no fun to be around. In fact, many like that land in mental asylums.

Another evil spirit may drive one to do a crime. Then, when the owner Soul of that human body sits

Walk the middle path, being aware to not stray from it too far to the left or right.

Ways I walk the middle path:

> This is a warring universe. To survive here, one must know its ways.

Write your thoughts about competition and spirituality:

in prison, the entity may leave to look for more action, for another sucker playing with a Ouija board.

It's all fun and games for an evil spirit.

Ouija boards, séances, and automatic handwriting are all like loaded guns in the hands of children.

From a spiritual point of view, no highly developed spiritual being would allow another entity to take away his liberty. But that's just what a Ouija board sets the stage to do. What advanced individual would risk the loss of freedom?

Do yourself a favor: put the Ouija board in the trash. It's a deadly "toy," the same as schoolyard drugs. Don't be a sucker of the negative power.

Is Competition Unspiritual?

Is it unspiritual to like games such as chess, since the very nature of such games is based on war, power, and egotistical competition?

Not in my opinion. This is a warring universe. To survive here, one must know its ways.

Chess is simply another way an individual can test his survival instinct. Competition is not necessarily a bad activity. It forms the very basis of many societies today. Their members must know how to move in such an environment and how to provide a protective shield (a home, for example) for themselves and their families.

Competition is all right as long as a person develops and follows a code of fair play.

Choosing the Words You Speak

What happens to those who use foul language? I hear it all the time at school, and I want to understand the consequences of it.

Foul language, no matter how you spell it, is for the barnyard. The simple ECK principle is this: where your attention is, so are you.

What you hold in your thoughts is what you become. Since you're an expression of the Sound and Light of God, do you want to bring beauty, joy, love, and harmony to the world? Then choose words that do that.

The words you speak are an expression of what you are and what you'd like to be.

Peer Pressure

Some youth feel they are missing something if they don't experience some of the things teenagers do (e.g., sex, drugs, rock and roll). What suggestions would you have to combat this peer pressure and keep your focus on God?

Average people try to pull exceptional people down to their own level. It's the herd instinct.

What about Smoking?

What do bad habits like smoking, drinking, etc., do to our spiritual bodies? Does this halt our spiritual advancement?

Yes. It riddles your aura with holes, to allow negative currents in. It destroys good judgment.

The Consequences of Drugs

As a teen, I wonder, Where is one when one is on drugs?

Drugs are a rose-lined lane to misery and unhappiness. I can't say this strongly enough.

Few who dabble in drugs want to admit that there is any danger in using them. They use them to escape

The words you speak are an expression of what you are and what you'd like to be.

Words I can say that will express what I'd like to be:

Soul Travel is the natural way for expansion of consciousness and travel into the spiritual worlds of God.

My spiritual insights:

boredom, and boredom itself is a crime against the creative power of Soul.

Every act has a consequence, so are we ready to pay the piper?

Drugs bring unreal experiences in the elementary Astral world—some good, some bad, but all petty. What good ever comes from putting our sanity on the line for little pills and powders?

How do you say no to "friends" who push drugs at you? That happened to me in a house where I once lived with thirteen other people. I just said no. God Consciousness was my goal, and I did not want to turn into a druggie like them.

Have you ever noticed the cute names the negative force has put on drugs? You know most of them—angel dust, coke, buttons, smack or horse, orange sunshine, and the like. The cute labels are to hide the horror that catches Soul once It falls for them. Drugs are a shortcut to more unbearable incarnations, and they hardly bring more than simple light and color, at best.

Chant HU if you want to see the negative force's face behind the face of a "friend" who pushes drugs at you. Soul Travel is better—it puts you in control of your life and is completely safe. Soul Travel is the natural way for expansion of consciousness and travel into the spiritual worlds of God.

Alcohol

Why and how does alcohol affect spiritual development?

What we eat and drink is our own business, of course.

An athlete who wants to compete in the Olympics must train hard, which means doing what is good for his body in every way. My guess is that few top athletes drink alcohol.

If you want God-Realization, you must train too. Alcohol dulls the senses. In my youth, I drank beer because it was a part of my German upbringing. But Paul Twitchell said that alcohol would hold me back spiritually. So after my Second Initiation, I quit drinking it.

It always feels good to rise in the morning with a clear mind—and to stay clearheaded all day.

The path of Eckankar can lift you into a higher state of consciousness. But alcohol? Unless a doctor has you take it for some treatment, it will only drop you into a lower state and keep you there.

What sort of choice is that?

The Choice Is Yours

My ex-boyfriend used to drink from time to time, and when I would see him the next day, I would be affected by it. I know there was a strong bond between us since he was the man I loved, so his drinking would unbalance me. Can you tell me how I can shield myself against the secondhand effects of alcohol and drugs, please?

The only way to shield yourself is to get such things out of your life. But the choice is yours. Situations seldom are so cut and dried, though, especially when someone we love dearly suddenly takes up drinking, drugs, smoking, cursing, lying, or some other habit.

What do you do then?

An example from my own life with smoking: A friend of many years smokes several packs of cigarettes a day. In the last few years, I've become very sensitive to smoke. So when my friend wanted to visit

The path of Eckankar can lift you into a higher state of consciousness.

What this means to me:

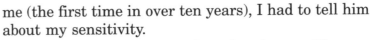

> Each human life *is* a precious gift of God. Be respectful of all life, especially your own.

How is your life precious to you?

me (the first time in over ten years), I had to tell him about my sensitivity.

We'd not be able to visit in a closed room. The smoke in his clothing would cause a serious health reaction for me. Believe me, it was a hard letter to send.

We remain friends. But all our correspondence must be in writing or by phone. Life gives us some hard choices.

When Someone Commits Suicide

On this journey home to God, we are sometimes faced with painful experiences. During these times, some youth make the choice to end their life. What is the spiritual lesson and responsibility in making that choice? How can we protect ourselves and be in tune with the Mahanta's guidance? And as youth and leaders in the world, how do we respond?

Life often is pain. If not physical pain, then surely emotional or mental dis-ease of some sort. Earth is God's boot camp for Souls.

Youth who take their lives are to be pitied only because they threw away on a whim the divine blessing of this life. In Christianity, it would be a final tragedy. The reason is that its belief system admits but to a single human existence in eternity and to lightly gamble it away is to forever suffer eternal damnation.

The teachings of Eckankar view human life on a broader scale. Each human life *is* a precious gift of God. After all, survival is one of our key teachings. Life is to cherish. Be respectful of all life, especially your own.

When someone commits suicide, it's due to ignorance or a willful disobedience of spiritual law. That person has made a shortsighted choice. The spiritual hierarchy will require that Soul to make amends in another human life, and another, under much more trying conditions. Finally, that Soul learns that suicide is no answer. Just another problem.

You will show love and compassion to the survivors.

How Important Is Our Diet?

How important is diet to spirituality?

Not important at all, IF . . . (Note the big *if.*)

If the foods in your diet let you feel and act with love, charity, and wisdom, then diet makes no difference at all to your spirituality.

But if a certain food, like a caffeine-loaded soft drink, makes you edgy or short-tempered, then you are sure to make some negative karma for yourself. That, of course, will hold you back spiritually.

Or if you like foods saturated with fat, like too many pizzas or hamburgers, and they let you put on too much weight. No problem spiritually if you're happy with the few extra pounds. A problem occurs though if the added weight upsets you. Do you then have a low opinion of yourself? If so, your attitude would hold you back spiritually.

So eat and drink what you please. If you find that some food or beverage is bringing you unhappiness or sickness, ask the Mahanta to help you control it.

The Challenge of Anorexia

Last year I struggled my way through anorexia. I thought that I was fully over it until just recently when I began to throw up my food. I am too scared to tell anyone and do not want to become bulimic.

How can I just accept my body and stop the eating disorders altogether?

If the foods in your diet let you feel and act with love, charity, and wisdom, then diet makes no difference at all to your spirituality.

Record what you eat today:

How did you feel?

Many an illness is due to eating a food that is wrong for us.

Foods that are wrong for me:

Foods that help me feel stronger spiritually:

To make a long answer short, I suggest you read *The Healing Power of Illness: The Meaning of Symptoms and How to Interpret Them* by Thorwald Dethlefsen and Rudiger Dahlke, M.D. Look in the index for anorexia nervosa.

The book takes a hard look at the condition.

How to Take Better Care of Yourself

Why do children get colds, headaches, and other illnesses?

It might sound funny, but children get sick for the same reasons that grown-ups do.

An illness may be left over from a past life. It shows up in this lifetime as a certain food that a person cannot eat. Sometimes, a child gets sick from a pet with fur.

Many an illness is due to eating a food that is wrong for us. I used to hate milk when I was young, because of the chunks of cream that floated on top. Yet I needed the calcium in dairy foods to grow strong teeth and bones. So I ate a lot of cheese. Of course, I didn't know that my head was always stuffed up because I was allergic to dairy foods.

Most times our body gets sick, it's trying to tell us something: to eat foods, wear clothes, or do some other thing that is better for us.

As you get older and learn more, you'll be able to help take better care of yourself.

Illness as Karma

I am eight years old. I think the ECK, Divine Spirit, knew I was going to do something wrong before I did it. So I got sick to pay for my future karma. Can this happen?

Yes, it can. If you know that thoughts are real, it should make you think twice before even thinking of doing wrong.

Most of our illnesses, though, are from something we've done in the past—such as eating too much of a certain food that our particular body cannot digest. At your age, I ate as much candy, cake, or pie as possible, because I never truly believed they would hurt me. They did.

You'll do better all around if you take it a little easy in everything. Enjoy yourself, but also understand that the responsibility to help or harm yourself, either physically or spiritually, rests mainly in your hands.

So first ask the Mahanta inwardly about the right way to act. Your life can then become easier and far richer in more ways than you could ever imagine.

The True Healer

How do you heal people, Wah Z?

The true healer is the ECK, Divine Spirit. When a healing takes place, it is through the power of the ECK. I don't take credit myself.

This question raises another: If one person is healed of a problem, why not all people?

The reason is that a healing depends a lot upon one's opening his heart to love. When some people need a healing, they think only about their love for Wah Z. They love him more than their illness. A miracle then occurs.

Even more important, they are willing not to have a healing, because they know that their illness is for a reason. It is helping them grow spiritually.

They'd be just as happy without a cure just so they knew the Master loved them as much as they love him.

And he does.

> The true healer is the ECK, Divine Spirit. When a healing takes place, it is through the power of the ECK.

Write about a time you received a healing.

> The youth, like a foolish fledgling, wants to *suddenly* be out on his own. But it's a cold, harsh world out there.

What I have learned by being in my family:

Did I Choose My Family?

Did you spiritually choose me to be with a family in Eckankar, or was it random?

That's an interesting question. It's the same one that troubled me after coming into Eckankar, and many other young or new ECKists grapple with it. It applies to non-ECK families too.

Frankly, yours is another version of the question, "Are you really my parents? Or did you adopt me?"

If the question does come up, it's often when an individual is ten to fourteen. The child begins to have his own thoughts and opinions. Just as likely, he chafes at some duty or discipline from a parent to teach him the acceptable ways of the society he's born into. His education is the parent's responsibility, though.

Yet the youth sees longer and stronger feathers on his wings. (Or a boy may triumphantly spot a couple of long hairs on his chin where he hopes the whiskers of manhood will soon sprout.) Maybe his feathers are long enough already to allow flights from the home nest? He thinks so.

That's where the question and a problem arise. His ideas, those of a fully dependent child, start to clash with those of his parent, whom divine law has given the job of educator. The youth is becoming less dependent now.

So the youth, like a foolish fledgling, wants to *suddenly* be out on his own. But it's a cold, harsh world out there. Much harder than he's ready for.

To answer your question, the choice of your family was partly your own and partly your family's, and then approved by the Mahanta, the Inner Master, for spiritual reasons. This choice of family was not random.

Yes, you're in a good family. It will now take five to seven years for you to learn how to fully grow into the duties and responsibilities expected of you in our society. Your parents can make this transition easier on you. They've been around the block a few times. So listen and learn. The easy way.

Taking Care of This World

Every so often, I hear ECK chelas make excuses for not taking social responsibility. They say they are detached from the physical plane.

The physical plane, they claim, is temporal and that our ultimate goal is spiritual unfoldment into the God Worlds.

I know that is true.

Yet is it not part of our spiritual duty to be responsible in society and toward our environment, and to help out in the immediate global crises?

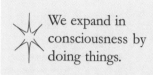

We expand in consciousness by doing things.

You're 100 percent right. People who write off this world as temporal think it's a worthless place and so miss out on a lot of valuable unfoldment. Like a child, they mess up their room and then expect their dad or mom to clean up after them. People who won't do their part in taking care of this world are like small children. They need to grow up.

How do they think one reaches God-Realization? It's not by hiding from the world, but by swimming in life. We expand in consciousness by doing things. How can anyone hope to grow spiritually and still keep an arm's length away from everyday life?

Do what you can to unfold, and let such people be. Sooner or later, they'll catch on.

List some things you do that help expand your consciousness.

Pockets of golden opportunities dot the earth. Everything is of the ECK (Holy Spirit).

Find a golden opportunity and write or draw it here:

Career Choice

I am trying to decide about a future career and an outer goal that is right for me. I was wondering how important a college education is today. Will attaining all of that mental knowledge affect my spiritual unfoldment? Also, does God care what one does in regard to a career, or is that up to the individual Soul? Is there some way I can tap into what God wants me to do?

How important is college today? It depends upon where you live and your cultural background. Pockets of golden opportunities dot the earth. Everything is of the ECK (Holy Spirit). We live where we do because of what there is to learn there.

Allow yourself a lot of breathing room when picking a career. If you lock on to a certain profession too soon, you will miss many chances to grow spiritually. Yet in the meantime learn all you can, no matter where you live. Learn for the joy of it. If your goal is purely to get rich, you will box yourself into a dull life.

Times and conditions change for each generation. A secret I've found that always helped for promotion was to do as well as I could in everything. Success has a way of finding those who always do their best.

God just wants you to become a Co-worker. You can be that anytime and in any place.

Is a Job Just a Job?

In doing what we love and loving what we do, are there jobs that don't help us spiritually? If so, why? And what can we do about it?

If two people love what they do but one is evil and the other is good, what would you expect of each?

At the national level, the first might love being a dictator or tyrant, while the second would be viewed as a wise, bold leader. At the neighborhood level, the evil-hearted one might love being a thief. The other, a doctor. At the family level, the first might like cruelty or argument, while the other opts for peace and reconciliation.

So, a job is a job is a job.

What makes the difference is what lies in an individual's heart.

Life, of course, is not so simple. Is anyone on earth all good or all evil? No, everyone is somewhere in between.

So there may be a Robin Hood whose stolen goods go, in part, to charity. Again, a doctor who gives unnecessary treatments to feed his bank account. Little is black or white, good or evil, pure justice or injustice—due to the influence of karma.

Free will is, therefore, an important element. Yet it rises from an individual's state of consciousness, because past experience whispers advice about the merits or risks of a course of action.

With all the above at play, you do know what jobs are good for you. Follow your heart. Learn the spiritual lessons in any given job. Then move on to a new challenge. So, a job is a job is a job. Your love and attention bring it to life, though, so stay with one—through thick and thin—until you've learned all it can teach you.

> Follow your heart. Learn the spiritual lessons in any given job. Then move on to a new challenge.

Spiritual lessons I am learning in my job:

Walk the Talk

What is the limit of responsibility in our daily life? I'm referring to our responsibility for the results from our own actions. For example, if we purchase a product that has been produced by a company that treats its workforce unfairly or restricts their freedom, to what level are we responsible for this by supporting such a company? This also includes poor treatment of animals and unnecessary damage to the environment.

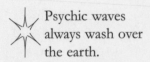

Psychic waves always wash over the earth.

My spiritual insights:

Psychic waves always wash over the earth. A common feature of people out to save the earth is their duplicity.

For example, there are accounts of environmentalist tours to a lovely place that ended with trash littering the landscape. Those are dishonest people.

Another example is people who rail against auto pollution but own and drive SUVs or large, expensive cars. Or also, environmental advocates who preach the development of the inner cities, while they live out in the country on large, sweeping estates. They are dishonest people.

They don't walk the talk.

Of course, such people often command a large group of followers who are the willing voices, hands, and feet of carrying forth the environmental message.

Look also at the proponents of electric cars. No pollution! Sounds good, doesn't it? But how to charge a car's batteries? With power created by fossil fuels or nuclear generators, since solar and wind power can supply but a fraction of our society's need for electricity to power lights, TVs, air conditioning, computers, etc.

Cars cause pollution? Horses in cities once resulted in city blocks reserved for manure piles stacked high. Flies.

Global warming? The largest contributors seldom spoken of are solar bursts and volcanic eruptions under the seas. Scientists are only now discovering the frequency with which the latter occur.

On the other hand, a clean planet is like a clean body. It's a noble cause to help get and keep it clean, but be careful of emotional entanglements from the psychic, emotional, waves that also pollute the earth.

Stay True to Your Mission

When making important choices that will deter-mine a lot of my life experiences, how can I know that I am following my highest inner guidance?

For example, how can I find the career that aligns with my spiritual destiny, but provides me with stabil-ity and security? Or in choosing a mate, how do I know if the relationship is going to grow into a future of the highest love? So my question is: How do you really get inner guidance, understand it enough to trust it, and have the discipline to follow it?

If you stay true to your mission in life, which is to become a Co-worker with God, the Holy Spirit and the Mahanta will guide you to the right places in life.

The real question is: How can one keep on track toward that mission? By the faithful practice of the Spiritual Exercises of ECK.

Now, it helps to understand a few things.

Just because you keep it in mind that life is trying to help you become a Co-worker with God doesn't mean that life will necessarily be easy. That depends upon your spiritual needs.

But know that no government or human estab-lishment can ever deliver on the vain promise to provide people with security from the cradle to the grave. That's not the purpose of life. There is no stability or security on earth. Any doubts? Study history to see how people manage to harm each other in wars, on the streets, and in the courts. That's life.

Few spiritual seekers ever fall into a lifetime career on the first try. Free will plays a major role in our future.

That extends even to choosing a mate. Both people in the relationship must do their best to love and build up their mate. If one or both of them fail at this, the relationship comes to hard times.

> Stay true to your mission in life by the faithful practice of the Spiritual Exercises of ECK.

What choices are you facing today that affect your mission?

To get true inner guidance, give God, the Mahanta, and yourself the purest love. And do your spiritual exercises in the same spirit of love.

Workbook:
Spiritual Choices

Key Insights
from This Chapter

- You can choose to be a Co-worker with God.

- Identify your personal and spiritual goals.

- Stay true to yourself and your mission.

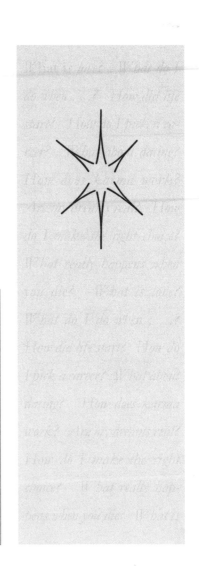

My key insights:

Spiritual Exercises to Explore These Insights

1. How can you discover why you are here? What do you think
    your mission is in this life? God works through what we love.
    Make a list of ten things you love to do.

    1. _____   6. _____

    2. _____   7. _____

    3. _____   8. _____

    4. _____   9. _____

    5. _____   10. _____

    Now pick three of these that are your favorites. How do they
    help you identify what you really want to do and your mission
    in this life?

    Write your insights here:

2. Think of three people who inspire you to be a good person. These are people who walk the talk in their life. They can be friends, teachers, family members, or someone from your religion. What have you learned from them about making difficult choices in their lives? How has the Holy Spirit guided them to the right places in life?

Write your insights here:

3. The ECK (Holy Spirit) will bring you many right seasons for spiritual growth. Imagine you are living a full life of love and service to God and others. What gives you the most happiness and brings you closest to God?

    Write what you see here:

4. If you like, reread "Identify Your Purpose" near the beginning of this chapter. Then reread or skim your two favorite books or short stories. Ask yourself, Are these two books or short stories plot-driven or character-driven? How do the characters make choices and what is the result? Write your insights on the similarities or differences here:

5. Before you go to sleep at night, ask the Mahanta inwardly about the right way to act, so your life can become easier and richer in more ways than you can imagine. Write or sketch details from any dreams you remember here:

6. You are Soul, here to learn spiritual lessons every day. What have you learned about yourself as you read this chapter?

The spiritual
exercises are
a good habit.
Like a student
remembering to
lock valuables in
a school locker, it
avoids trouble.

6

THE SPIRITUAL EXERCISES OF ECK

Golden Key to Life

Often I have distractions in life, school, relationships, etc., that make it hard to keep myself disciplined. What advice do you have for the youth to help them keep focused and disciplined with their spiritual exercises? Also, some youth have difficulty just sitting still. Are there active ways to do spiritual exercises?

The whole purpose of distractions is to throw your attention off the ECK, the Holy Spirit. Discipline is what you came here to learn.

You rightly make the connection between a focused discipline and the spiritual exercises. The exercises are the golden key to a life of meaning and happiness.

Are there active ways to do the spiritual exercises? Sure, a lot of them.

For younger children, say, "Shut your eyes a minute. Imagine there's a piece of white paper in front of you and all the colors you need are beside it.

> The exercises are the golden key to a life of meaning and happiness.

Draw a big flower. Done? OK, now draw a happy face on it. That's the Mahanta. Listen, did he tell you something special?"

Whatever spiritual exercise you create, be sure that it lets the child be an actor in it. The child must have the lead role in the theater of his spiritual exercise.

The ECK teachings, you see, help people on their own path home to God. So each person is the star in his own world.

Read on to learn about the Spiritual Exercises of ECK and get tips on ways to do them.

What Are Spiritual Exercises?

What is the purpose of Eckankar's spiritual exercises? Will they take me where I want to go spiritually?

The whole focus of Eckankar is direct experience of the Light and Sound of God. This can come through practice of the Spiritual Exercises of ECK.

Different spiritual exercises are given in the Eckankar books, especially *The Spiritual Exercises of ECK.* Simply try them, and see if they work. Don't push yourself, though. There's no reason to.

If you are successful with the spiritual exercises, you ought to become aware of either the Light or Sound of God. You also might meet the Inner Master, the Mahanta, who always awaits the individual who is sincere in seeking truth.

Some people have quite an active inner life and travel widely in the inner worlds; others are quite content to let Divine Spirit guide them indirectly in their daily lives. Let any teaching you are studying fit you instead of trying to adapt to something that is not comfortable.

Take your whole lifetime to make up your mind if you want. After all, it is your life.

The ECK teachings help people on their own path home to God. So each person is the star in his own world.

Ways I am a star in my own world:

Benefits of Spiritual Exercise

How can I get the most out of my spiritual exercises? What should I be learning from them?

If you eat the same food every day for two weeks, it can get pretty dull. You may enjoy it the first day, and the second day is all right. But by the second week, you're tired of it. So you experiment; you experiment with something new.

It's the same with the spiritual exercises. You experiment with them; you try new things. You're in your own God Worlds. I've gone to different extremes with the exercises, trying very complicated ones I developed for myself, dropping them when they didn't work anymore.

It's like a vein of gold running through a mountain. You're on it for a while, then the vein runs out and you have to scout around and find another one.

Are we learning something new every day from what we're doing? Are we getting insight and help from the inner? This is what we ought to be working for.

How can we face life as we find it? The key is always through the Spiritual Exercises of ECK.

Inner Experiences

In my spiritual exercises, I get direct information about what's needed in the moment. But these aren't grand inner experiences. Is this just a passing phase?

Is there a technique I could do to be a more conscious explorer of the Far Country?

There is a way to be more aware of your travels in the higher worlds. You must train your mind to recall details. This means developing the power of your imagination, which is a lot harder than it sounds, but there is an enjoyable way to go about it.

> Are we learning something new every day from what we're doing?

What I am learning today:

Living in the moment means integrating the lessons of yesterday into the actions of today.

How I am integrating the lessons of yesterday into my actions today:

Do you play golf? Let's say you have trouble with a slice. You can work out that problem both here in the physical and on the inner planes.

Get a book by a golf pro that shows ways to correct a slice. Study the exact methods given. Then, when you lie down for the night or while at rest some other time, imagine yourself on a golf course. Now practice the expert's advice—all in your imagination. Address the ball, hit it in the proper way, and watch it fly straight down the fairway. Do this again and again. Pay attention to your grip, your stance, and the position of your arms and head.

If you are a golfer, you'll like this exercise. It works with any sport.

Your game will improve, but more important, you'll soon find it easier to recall your journeys into the higher worlds of God.

Spiritual Exercises Help You Live in the Moment

How can the Spiritual Exercises of ECK help me live in the moment? What does it really mean to live in the moment?

The basis of the ECK teachings is experience. All that we can ever know depends upon either our own experiences or those of others.

But experience is far from being a spiritual cure-all. Much of it is learning the same old thing over and over again, because we don't accept prior lessons into our state of consciousness. And so, old lessons repeat. This refusal or inability to learn is what karma and reincarnation are all about.

So an ECKist does not want to spin his wheels. Nor should he ever have to.

Living in the moment means integrating the lessons of yesterday into the actions of today. Yes, an ECKist does make plans. He makes plans to arrange his affairs so they run as smoothly as possible. He allots his time to activities which benefit him and others.

Now, how does he avoid getting sucked into the whirlpool that catches the unwary traveler and brings on destruction?

Simple. He practices the Spiritual Exercises of ECK each day. He sings a holy name of God or the ECK while he is up and about. These are the right actions. They push back the prison of the human consciousness and let in the Light and Sound of God. The spiritual exercises prepare a warm and friendly place in the heart for the Mahanta to stay.

Living in the moment, then, depends upon experience taken to heart in the right way.

Much of the experience of people on the wheel of death and rebirth is *unconscious* experience. So they run in a circle. The Spiritual Exercises of ECK, however, lead to *conscious* experience. They go in the most direct way to God in the Ocean of Love and Mercy.

Creating a Good Habit

Do you ever get really frustrated with ECKists who don't do their spiritual exercises? I know you are the Master, but you are also human, so does that ever affect you?

I let all Souls go at their own pace. Yes, it is clear when an individual is making problems by forgetting to do the ECK Spiritual Exercises. It's part of learning.

The spiritual exercises are a good habit, like a student remembering to lock valuables in a school locker. It avoids trouble.

The practice of the exercises forms a pact with the Master. By doing them, an individual says, "Please help me work out my karma and find God." Then the

The spiritual exercises are a good habit, like a student remembering to lock valuables in a school locker. It avoids trouble.

Ways the spiritual exercises help me:

Master lets unnecessary karma burn off without the chela (spiritual student) having to live through it.

It makes life more pleasant and meaningful.

So you see, there is a real advantage for chelas who do their spiritual exercises.

Degree of Spiritual Protection

If someone slacks off on their spiritual exercises for a period of time, does he or she still have the guidance of the Mahanta? Can one still be in touch with Divine Spirit at this time?

Let me answer you like this: One day in late spring I took a walk near a pond. The sun was very hot. On the edge of the grass by the water stood a duck. Under her were three ducklings using her for a sunscreen.

Someone on the path of ECK who neglects the spiritual exercises is like a duckling who leaves the protection of its mother. He is ignoring the guidance of the Master. His contact with the Light and Sound of ECK will only be a small part of what it was before.

When the sun of karma gets too hot for comfort, like the duckling, he can run back to his sunscreen— the Mahanta. The run back is the spiritual exercise.

Practice and Repetition

I find it hard to ask questions during my spiritual exercises and then listen for answers. Please, can you tell me the best way to listen and get answers without my mind going to other places causing distraction?

The answers may not come during contemplation. Often they come later in the day or week. But they do come.

Your mind, like the minds of many others, likes to jump around. It's unable to focus on one thing. The Mahanta does give you answers in contemplation but

---

The Master lets unnecessary karma burn off without the chela (spiritual student) having to live through it.
It makes life more pleasant and meaningful.

New good habits I want in my life:

they get lost in a sea of other answers, creations of your mind.

But read on. There is a way to overcome the play of mind.

Once in a grocery store I complimented the woman at the checkout stand on how fast she could identify the many different greens and vegetables in plastic bags, and then punch the right codes into the computer. She was as fast as an automatic scanner. She was modest about her skills.

"Practice and repetition," she said. "Practice and repetition."

It's the same with the Spiritual Exercises of ECK. It takes practice and repetition. Before long, the mind will behave and stop acting like a spoiled child, for that's what it is. It's used to having its own way.

But if you practice the spiritual exercises on a regular schedule, like a meal, you'll get the inner nourishment you seek.

Learning How to Concentrate

I do not know how to concentrate. When I want to contemplate on a certain subject, I lose control and start thinking of anything. Do you have any suggestions that could help me?

Paul Twitchell, the modern-day founder of Eckankar, once wrote that the mind likes to jump around like a monkey.

First of all, don't worry about it.

Second, entertain your mind during the Spiritual Exercises of ECK. Do an exercise a slightly different way each time. Let the mind play. Remember who is watching your mind play: the real you (Soul). Come to that realization during your spiritual exercise, and you will realize that Soul Itself is calm and doesn't jump around.

Do an exercise a slightly different way each time. Let the mind play.

Try a spiritual exercise in a new way. What did you experience?

The spiritual exercise can help you learn the ways of ECK in our world. That includes learning what's right or wrong.

What I am learning about right and wrong from the spiritual exercises:

It's hard to get the mind absolutely still. But by suddenly knowing that you, the watcher (Soul), are still, the antics of the mind won't upset you anymore.

After all, the mind jumps around to upset you. Does this help you?

Why Discipline Yourself?

In the Eckankar books I read about self-discipline, true contemplation of the ECK works, and complete inner reliance on the Mahanta. What do these terms really mean?

Sometimes people (and you) see yourself as going against the grain. You too often like to do it your way, regardless of the thoughts and feelings of others.

Such a budding independence of thought occurs to many of us at your age. We know a little and jump the gun. It's perfectly obvious to us that we know it all and should have a bigger role in decisions that affect us. That's all fine, but isn't it the ego on a rampage? Much trouble lies down that road.

So how does an ECK chela tie in self-discipline to true contemplation?

A daily contemplation (it only has to be five minutes at going to sleep or upon arising) can control a wild ego, our little self. The spiritual exercise can help you learn the ways of ECK in our world. That includes learning what's right or wrong.

Then what does complete inner reliance on the Mahanta mean?

The short spiritual exercises done twice a day will slap a bridle on a runaway, wild ego. In plain language you can learn to admit to wrong thoughts and opinions. It's a big step. Then the Mahanta's voice can come through the fog of your human consciousness to show you an easier way in your spiritual life.

So self-discipline is the key to a spiritual life. It's the gateway to a true contemplation of the ECK works.

That, in turn, lets you hear the Mahanta's voice.

You correctly named the three key parts to leading a true spiritual life. But now the ball's in your court.

Act "As If"

If I ask for you as the Mahanta to be with me, how do I know you are really there or if it is just me pretending you are there?

A skeptic would say there's no way to know.

And so might some people who've been in Eckankar since babyhood, since they grew up with the presence of the Mahanta and have come to take it for granted.

If all is pretty nearly going well for you, pay more attention to your dreams, your spiritual exercises, and the little "coincidences" that gently flow in and out of your life. Not just to the ones that turn out in your favor. But look also for the moments when a little thing seems to go wrong for you—yet teaches or reminds you of what is right or wrong.

Those little incidents will be examples of the Mahanta's presence. There is also a spiritual principle that you are already doing: "Act as if." For example, if you want the Mahanta in your life as a spiritual guide, act as if he is.

He is anyway, of course, but it will help you to stay aware of his presence.

Now, this is earth, a school for Soul's spiritual education. It is much better at teaching people than any public or private school. The lessons and tests of

"Act as if." For example, if you want the Mahanta in your life as a spiritual guide, act as if he is.

Act as if. What did you learn? What happened?

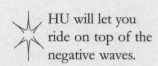

HU will let you ride on top of the negative waves.

Sing HU and imagine riding on top of the negative waves. What is it like?

spiritual living will crop up around you at any and all times, unsuspected as such.

Sometimes it will be the Kal, the negative force, whispering through your closest friend, "Ah, smoke it. One puff won't hurt."

That's a test. To pass it, remember to act "as if" and ask, "What should I do, Mahanta?" Guess. Friends once said that to me. I said, "I don't need it."

Keep your eyes and heart open. I *am* always with you.

Learning Flexibility

When I do my spiritual exercises or sing HU, sometimes I feel like I can't keep going. It's so hard for me to sing for a good amount of time or to do a full spiritual exercise. Why do I have such a difficult time concentrating, and what can I do about it?

You wrote this question while a student in Spain. The country has a strong Catholic tradition. That centuries-old tradition is like a radio station broadcasting radio waves to all corners of Spain.

Those waves rise from the Astral Plane. They will try to cause interference with the spiritual practices of other religions.

So, do more short spiritual exercises. Fit them into a new rhythm of living. Ebb and flow with the psychic currents, but ride on top of them. There's a way to do that. Sing HU but once when there's a need. Let HU fill your heart, though.

HU will let you ride on top of the negative waves.

The time in Spain is a good opportunity to learn flexibility with the Spiritual Exercises of ECK.

Fit the spiritual exercises to you, instead of you to them.

My book *The Spiritual Exercises of ECK* gives dozens of them. The great number are a means of teaching ECK chelas (spiritual students) to be flexible. After all, life flows. So must we. That means in every department of our life.

No, flexibility does not include bending the spiritual laws. Rather, we learn to move around blocks, because life provides a way around them.

Did you ever watch a leaf floating downstream in a brook? It will catch on a twig, then free itself. Then, on with the journey.

My love and thoughts are with you on your journey.

The Personal Mantra

I don't feel anything when I chant my special word. Could I be doing something wrong? How does Soul link up with the ECK (Holy Spirit) through mantrams?

The personal mantram has no power but by the Mahanta, the Inner Master. The special word fits an individual's rate of vibration and is the tuning fork that makes him in tune with the ECK. The ECK is one and the same, but each Soul is at a different level of consciousness. The word attunes one to the ECK.

Please do not become discouraged by your apparent inability to have any experiences during contemplation. Your special word is like a spiritual vitamin that builds one's inner strength over a certain length of time. Deep changes occur in you when you chant your word. Karma is dissolved from the lower bodies until the weight on Soul is lightened. Then, when you are most relaxed in the serenity of the Mahanta's abiding presence, he will take you into the Sound and Light of God—which is your main goal at this time.

Within twelve months, you should find yourself suddenly in a new and joyful inner state that will prove to you once and for all that you are Soul, a spark of God.

> The special word fits an individual's rate of vibration and is the tuning fork that makes him in tune with the ECK.

> Imagine your special word is a vitamin you take every day to become spiritually stronger. Draw or write your insights here:

Keep in mind that a spiritual dance will bring a dancer into harmony with the rhythm of the divine Sound Current.

Try making up a spiritual dance. Draw or write about it here:

A Spiritual Dance

I am a dancer, and I wonder if there could be (or ever has been) Spiritual Exercises of ECK in movement? I know about the systems like yoga, tai chi, or certain forms of martial arts, but they seem to be rooted in other spiritual paths and therefore appear not to aim at experiences with the pure Light and Sound. Is this possible with physical exercises, or do they just aim for physical health (or art, as in dance)?

The whirling dervishes of Persia, a Muslim sect, danced until reaching a trance state, where they enjoyed the bliss of Allah. Their dance was a spiritual exercise.

Neoplatonists of ancient Greece, followers of Plato, felt that a sacred dance would allow for the sudden arrival of God, who'd then take part. Whatever the sacred dance, it was often performed in a circle around a center, to show how all life revolves around the Creator.

It's well to remember that ECK is the origin of all religions. Many ECK chelas were once members of them in past lives, so it's understandable that you and other dancers may wish for a spiritual exercise in a dance form.

Why not develop your own?

Keep in mind that a spiritual dance will bring a dancer into harmony with the rhythm of the divine Sound Current. It's a dance to open the heart. It will bring joy and produce a spirit of thanksgiving for the gift of life. And look for the dance to change.

Begin with a simple dance. The Mahanta will reveal new steps and movements as you unfold spiritually in your efforts to become one with ECK, the Holy Spirit.

Succeed at Soul Travel

I read about placing my attention on my Third Eye, above and between my eyebrows, during contemplation. But when I do this, it always begins to sway and move around. This makes me yawn and disturbs my spiritual exercise. Do you have any suggestions?

The mind gets bored fast. So if it makes you yawn when you place your attention on the Third Eye, then put it on your crown chakra instead. That's the top of your head. That spiritual center is actually the easiest place to succeed at Soul Travel.

Do You Have Dramatic Inner Experiences?

What can I do to get colorful, vivid, exciting, and dramatic inner experiences?

Those inner experiences you describe are usually Soul Travel. It takes a very strong desire to do it, unless the Mahanta gives you a special hand. People must want to Soul Travel very much, otherwise they won't develop themselves spiritually for the journey. The worlds of God can overwhelm people who are not prepared for them.

So how can you get these dramatic inner experiences? Start by doing your spiritual exercises every night before you go to bed. Then, develop methods to remember your dreams better by using a tape recorder or taking notes.

Invent new ways of doing the spiritual exercises given in the ECK discourses. Make them more dramatic and appealing, to fit you personally.

Invent new ways of doing the spiritual exercises. Make them more dramatic and appealing, to fit you personally.

My new personal spiritual exercise:

Leave the eye of Soul alert to the coming of the teacher. Look for me, because I am always with you.

Sing HU. Imagine your heart opening to God's love. Draw or write about it here:

Three Steps to Soul Travel

What instruction, advice, or technique would you give someone on how to sleep properly, so he can make use of the period when his body is stilled and leave it to travel in the upper regions with his teacher?

There are three main steps I recommend. First, arrange your schedule to get as much sleep as needed to be fresh in the morning.

Second, for a few minutes before sleeping, read from one of the Eckankar books to signal Soul of your intent to pursue spiritual activity during sleep.

Third, contemplate upon the face of the Mahanta, the Living ECK Master at bedtime. Do this in either a seated position or lying on your back. In the spiritual exercise, give an invitation to the Inner Master like this: "I welcome you into my heart as into my home. Please enter it with joy."

Then go to sleep as usual, but leave the eye of Soul alert to the coming of the teacher. Look for me, because I am always with you.

What the HU Does for You

What does the HU do?

It opens your heart to God, the ECK (Holy Spirit), and the Mahanta. In other words, HU opens you to God's sweet love.

Workbook:
The Spiritual Exercises of ECK

Key Insights
from This Chapter

- HU opens your heart to God's love.

- Live in the moment.

- Integrate the lessons of yesterday into today.

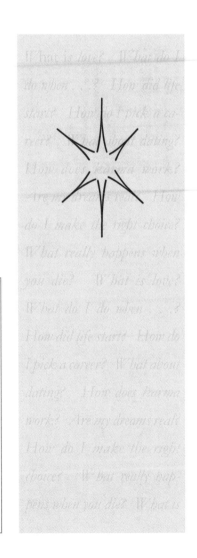

My key insights:

Spiritual Exercises to Explore These Insights

1. Practice a different spiritual exercise each day for one week. Use my book *The Spiritual Exercises of ECK* or this chapter for ideas, or make up your own. As Soul, you are a creative being. What kind of spiritual exercise do you enjoy the most? What do you like about it?

   Record your insights here:

2. Before sleep, give an invitation to the Inner Master like this: "I welcome you into my heart as into my home. Please enter it with joy." Then go to sleep as usual but leave the eye of Soul alert to the coming of the teacher. Write or draw any dream you remember here:

3. The Spiritual Exercises of ECK open your heart to God's love.
    What happens when you practice the spiritual exercises? How
    is your life different?

    Write your observations here:

4. Doing a spiritual exercise every day requires self-discipline. What benefits will this bring you?

Write your thoughts here:

When you do a spiritual exercise with love in your heart, it is both a way to express your love for God and to bring the blessings of God into your life. Practice a spiritual exercise every day for the next two weeks and record what happens here:

5. You are Soul, here to learn spiritual lessons every day. What have you learned about yourself as you read this chapter?

You must learn
to look for
opportunities
beyond your
present horizon.

7

SPIRITUAL FREEDOM

Can I Be Spiritual and Successful in Life?

I am confused about detachment and how it works in terms of striving for anything, or if we even should strive. Should a person try to get ahead or be successful in worldly terms, or should he just put his efforts into spiritual unfoldment (aside from supporting himself and dependents if he has them)? Is wanting, striving, and desiring just another negative trap?

The wrong definition for detachment is "don't get involved in life." In Eckankar, we are detached, but we are also great lovers of life. Can it be any other way for a Co-worker with God?

The path of Eckankar is only to enhance our spiritual growth. How does this unfoldment come about? Through daily duties. Yes, it is all right to set goals in business. We can set goals, work to accomplish them, and still be working in the arena of detachment. Detachment means that if our plans don't work out as we think they should, life won't crush us.

The path of ECK ought to bring a zest for life. Each activity contains within it the seed of a spiritual

We are detached, but we are also great lovers of life. Can it be any other way for a Co-worker with God?

167

> We must first give to life if we expect life to give anything in return. This is the divine law.

What do you give to life each day?

What do you receive in return?

lesson. We do not make spiritual progress by doing as little as possible in life. The individual must make an honest evaluation of his talents, interests, and training to decide what goals he wishes to strive for.

Every time he sets out to win small goals, he is aware in Soul consciousness that their only purpose is to give instruction in becoming a citizen of the spiritual hierarchy.

We must first give to life if we expect life to give anything in return. This is the divine law. Life presents a whole series of opportunities. These let us tap into the God Force for aid. This is achieved through the regular practice of the Spiritual Exercises of ECK.

What Must I Give Up?

What must I give up for spiritual freedom?

The only thing we give up to Divine Spirit is the inner direction of our spiritual affairs. This does not mean giving up family, friends, or earthly possessions. The Living ECK Master does not ask this of anyone.

The purpose of the path of ECK is simply to outline the most direct route back to the heart of God. The traps and pitfalls are outlined in the writings of ECK. Learning the invisible laws that affect our every act, whether or not we are conscious of them, will allow us to straighten out our life. We find that every aspect of our personal life begins to be smoother. This follows the principle: as above, so below.

Not everyone is willing to exercise the self-disciplines that are needed to overcome the downward pull of mind and matter and ascend toward the true regions of light. This should be their choice.

There are countless states of consciousness among the children of God on this planet. The Divine Essence has provided numerous religions to fit the needs of most of these Souls. Thus we recognize other religions as offshoots of ECK, Divine Spirit. Eckankar is not the only path to God, but it is the most direct.

The law of the universes is that one must pay in the true coin for everything received. The Light and Sound of God are generally reached by faithful practice of the Spiritual Exercises of ECK. Changes must often be made slowly in order to maintain a balance in everyday life.

The path of ECK is not for ascetics, but for those willing to walk the middle path of total responsibility toward God-Realization.

> The steps to spiritual freedom are these: (1) learn to love yourself, (2) learn to love others (human love), and (3) this will open your heart to love for God.

A Key to Spiritual Freedom

From a religious point of view, what is the importance of a physical relationship while obtaining spiritual freedom?

A physical relationship is the first step to loving God. Love unties the bonds that anchor us to the material world of wants and desires. So divine love leads directly to spiritual freedom.

The steps to spiritual freedom are these: (1) learn to love yourself, (2) learn to love others (human love), and (3) this will open your heart to love for God. That is the key to spiritual freedom.

Your journey to God begins at home.

Ways I can love myself:

Ways I can love others:

Ways I can love God:

About God Consciousness

Sometimes I think it would be lonely to have total awareness—all alone, learning but never reaching an end, a home.

There are days when I long to be rid of the lower worlds, but other times I am not sure that I would be happy. If you don't mind, would you please tell me

You can learn to see life clearly too. Do the Spiritual Exercises of ECK.

Try a different ECK spiritual exercise today. Write about it here:

when you reached the point in your life where you knew for sure that you wanted to continue learning into infinity and why. Also, what would one's goals be once he gained total awareness?

Actually, the Mahanta saw my deep desire for truth. He led me step-by-step because of my willingness to follow him. This led eventually to an experience told in my book *Autobiography of a Modern Prophet*.

It was on a bridge, with a stranger, that the limitations of my lower self were torn away. I felt alone, exposed, and afraid. And this was during the experience of God-Realization! Also in my book I treat some of the misconceptions that people carry about God Consciousness.

My goal now is simply to serve the Sugmad, as we call God in Eckankar. There is nothing else to do. Service to It is life, anything less is nothing.

See Life Clearly

Would you please explain to me why the Kal, the negative power, is in this physical world causing confusion for people?

It's his job.

People will find life confusing until they can open their Spiritual Eye, which sees through the plays of illusion the Kal throws over them like a hood. ECKists who are further ahead spiritually don't go around in a state of confusion from him anymore.

You can learn to see life clearly too. Do the Spiritual Exercises of ECK.

See through the Eyes of Soul

I know that we should not get caught up in the illusions of this physical world, but where is the middle ground of compassion and true understand-

ing? What is the spiritual reality of some of the situations of upheaval and change which are being experienced on the planet today?

You must first know what it really means to be detached from the world. It is a spiritual point of view that a person can adopt: to see through the eyes of Soul. In no way does it suggest a cold heart, as so many imagine.

What does it mean to be detached? It simply means to know that life does have a purpose, even when you can't see it in a given situation. Just be a channel for ECK, which is Love Itself. Then you'll find there is all kinds of room in this world for compassion and true understanding.

Why the upheaval in the world today? It is nothing new. Please begin your own study of history; then very little of what you hear about people will ever surprise you again.

Earth is often a kettle of boiling water, but it's still the best place for Soul to find the purity of being.

What does it mean to be detached? It is a spiritual point of view that a person can adopt: to see through the eyes of Soul.

How I see through the eyes of Soul:

Your Quest for God's Love

One day, I saw at least a hundred eagles circling the sky. It was a sight to behold. What is the spiritual symbolism of this experience?

The eagle is a symbol of spiritual principles, of Divine Spirit. It is a symbol of great significance to you.

To see a hundred eagles is a spiritual blessing, for it is the Mahanta's way of saying that you can reach new heights in your quest for God's love. But several things are needed.

> God created the lower worlds out of spiritual necessity. Each Soul was sent there to become more godlike in nature.

How I am becoming more godlike:

The eagle speaks of nobility, yet it requires one to put aside a fear of the unknown. In addition, it means the ability to accept all experiences in life, the good and the bad, and realize that they are to help you receive more divine love. You must also learn to look for opportunities beyond your present horizon.

Read more about the eagle in Paul Twitchell's *The ECK-Vidya, Ancient Science of Prophecy.*

Why Is There Suffering?

I do not understand animals killing each other cruelly in the jungle. If I was God and was all knowing, all seeing, and all powerful, why would I create a Soul which would need all these ugly experiences? Instead, I think I would create a world in which everybody is happy and knows all, without need for suffering. Please tell me why a "Loving Father" has such a gloomy plan.

In the pure world of Soul there is no death. Birth and death are both illusions of these lower worlds of matter, energy, space, and time. God put Soul in that perfect heaven above the Soul Plane, but It wasn't developing the God qualities of love and mercy.

So God created the lower worlds out of spiritual necessity. Each Soul was sent there to become more godlike in nature.

This process of karma and reincarnation is like the mill wheel that grinds exceedingly fine. Like it or not, that is the divine plan.

Yours is a good and honest question. The fact is that on our way to becoming a Co-worker with God, we do actually get a chance to create our worlds as we see fit. In everyday terms, it means we can make our home as pleasant as heaven. That means, of course, that we have to be pleasant too.

Put all God qualities like patience and love together in yourself, and you will be a joy to all who know you. In fact, you'll be one of those saints spoken of with reverence in the histories of religions.

What Happens after Death?

What happens to us after death?

I'll paint a picture of the afterlife with a broad brush. The reason is that consciousness is like a river of water in that it goes gradually from a small stream to a larger one.

A composer, for example, uses a similar method. When he wishes to move up, say, eleven notes from a starting note, he will work his way up in gradual steps rather than in one big leap. He may go up two notes, drop back a half note, move up a full note, and so on, until he reaches the eleventh note he was aiming for.

These gradual movements from the smaller to the larger or the lower to the higher are to prevent a destructive or jarring effect upon the sensibilities of man or nature.

So is it, too, when an individual moves from this life to the afterlife. It is within the limits of one's expectations.

Of course, we do not speak here about the particular event that causes death, such as an accident, other violence, or even a peaceful passing in bed after reaching a ripe old age. Our attention is upon what sort of life one can expect in the other worlds after his passing.

It will be similar to what an individual gains on earth and his spiritual state of consciousness. If he embraces the images and conditions of a Christian, he will start there in the continuation of his life in the other worlds.

Soul must use the earthly life to expand in consciousness via the Spiritual Exercises of ECK.

Soul must use the earthly life to expand in consciousness via the Spiritual Exercises of ECK.

How I am growing in consciousness:

> Your life today is the sum of all your past choices.

Think of a situation in your life you want more clarity with. Ask yourself, What is the spiritual purpose of this situation? What is life trying to teach me here? Record your insights:

These exercises open a person's heart to God's love, which is to help and comfort all. With this understanding, one may then become a real spiritual traveler. He begins his mission as a Co-worker with God. Everything is an open book. Life is a joyful, interesting, and useful one, of service to all.

Open Your Heart to Love Divine

If every day in my spiritual exercises I declare myself a true vehicle for God and during the course of the day I find myself in situations that don't look, seem, or feel right, what does that mean? Does it mean I need the experience for my spiritual development or that I am there to help others or that I made the wrong choice?

Every situation in your life has some spiritual purpose to it.

By doing the Spiritual Exercises of ECK every day, you open your heart and mind to the ECK, Holy Spirit, to give the experiences of most spiritual use to you.

As you've seen, not every experience is to your liking. Life is about making choices. The spiritual exercises open your awareness to see which of your decisions have a better outcome. Time and experience do teach us to make better long-term choices.

In a spiritual sense, there isn't an absolute right or wrong choice. But wait! Is that to say that anything goes? Not on your life.

The Law of Karma sees to that. Every choice, as you're learning, bears a consequence.

In a nutshell, your life today is the sum of all your past choices. So who's to blame for what? It all gets down to Number One—us—as the creator of our own fortunes and misfortunes.

Researchers have discovered two new decision centers in people other than in the head. These are the heart and intestines. That means, an individual would do well to make choices with something other than his head. He should also pay attention to "gut feelings" and to the whisperings of his heart.

Of course, these three minds receive messages from Soul. Imperfect choices mean incomplete experience. But isn't the gathering of experience the way to develop a greater degree of spiritual purity?

So, every experience is a teacher. Keep up with your spiritual exercises. They open your heart to love divine. Then all will benefit.

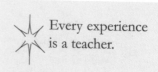 Every experience is a teacher.

What have your experiences taught you?

Cycle of Karma and Reincarnation

Please explain what happens to us as Soul when the physical body dies. How does karma come into play?

You, as an individual Soul, have a body on each of the inner planes—the emotional, causal, mental, and etheric (subconscious) levels. A body can only exist in a world, or plane, of like substance.

Now think of karma, whatever chunk of it happens to be on one plane or another, as a schoolbag full of books. Each chunk of karma, like one book, is like one part of a whole body of other karma (books).

This karma, as a collective whole, is all the lessons that Soul (a person) needs in order to become a more godlike being.

So when the physical body dies, any karma (like a book) not completely learned is put in the schoolbag and carried home (in this case, to the Astral Plane). There's homework between lives. It's a chance to review the day's (or past physical life's) lessons, take them to heart, and try to do better in (earth's) school tomorrow (the next lifetime in the Physical Plane—perhaps on earth again).

At death the main karma, by which an individual was learning the purity of spirit in an earlier life,

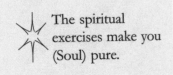

The spiritual exercises make you (Soul) pure.

Ways I am becoming pure:

moves to the plane above. At rebirth, all unlearned lessons of that karma continue.

There's a shortcut to this tiresome cycle of karma and reincarnation. The Mahanta, the Living ECK Master can show those with the eyes to see and the ears to hear a better way.

Much of one's karma in daily life can thus work off in the dream state. It's less wear and tear on the body.

Soul cares only for experience. Titles and position mean little to It, and Its desire to serve God results in the purest love of all.

Wheel of Awagawan

Does the Wheel of Awagawan ever end?

Yes, it does. The Wheel of Awagawan means an endless round of births and deaths. People go around the wheel many hundreds of times, and each time is one lifetime. They must meet the Mahanta, the Living ECK Master if they ever hope to get off it, though.

The Mahanta shows you how to do the Spiritual Exercises of ECK. They help you work off the karma that has kept you on the Wheel of Awagawan.

The spiritual exercises make you (Soul) pure.

When you become pure enough in this lifetime, you will never again have to return to earth unless you want to help others find spiritual freedom too. That's what the ECK Masters do.

Giving True Freedom

How can one remove ego when being a channel for Divine Spirit and give and receive without the little self becoming involved?

It's a battle that's never won as long as Soul lives in the physical world. We usually trip over ourselves when giving or receiving both human and divine love.

A friendship, for instance, may start on a high level. But once the two people begin to know each other better, the friendship is threatened when one gives a gift with strings attached. That's control, or power, trying to enter the relationship. See the ego at work?

Perhaps the hardest thing to learn is to offer a gift, but then to let the other freely accept it or not. This is nonattachment.

Our training to be a Co-worker with God occurs in the classroom of our daily life. The lessons are tedious at times, but always thorough.

> Our training to be a Co-worker with God occurs in the classroom of our daily life.

Spiritual Purpose of the Arts

What is the spiritual purpose of the arts: writing, painting, music, etc.?

This answer will come as a shock to some beginning artists and to many advanced ones as well. What is the spiritual purpose of the arts? It is to learn structure.

Until an artist has a very clear idea of how small units combine to make larger objects in God's worlds, he or she will never produce any great art.

Once an artist creates a true structure, then divine love can pour into it and make it a living thing of beauty.

Such a poem, painting, story, or piece of music by a master artist helps people escape the grip of this material world and taste the joy of spiritual freedom. So always look to see how the very smallest things around you make up bigger things.

A master artist is always a scientist first.

Spiritual Freedom and Patriotism

How do you feel about national patriotism?

This is a hard issue to address. When patriotism becomes blind emotion, it will steal people's freedom.

How God is training me to be a Co-worker in my daily life:

> We recognize the imperfection of life on earth, and we do fulfill our duties to the state. However, we're always mindful of our calling to God. It comes first.

Use this space for your journal:

Patriotism as a measured, rational thing is all right. It's nothing more than one's way of saying, "I like what my country is and what it stands for."

In Eckankar, we support every good government.

The United States is a product of the U.S. Constitution. It is the business plan, if you will, of the rights and responsibilities of U.S. citizens. That document was the creation of men who'd studied history and philosophy. They were not bumpkins.

Their research showed the abysmal result of earlier attempts at a republic. They had all failed.

Ancient Greece developed the idea, but its republic collapsed when it changed, in time, to a democracy. People voted themselves more and more public pay for normal civic duties. That burgeoning democracy fell upon its own sword.

When the republic had deteriorated into a near absolute democracy, its form of government became mob rule. It had surrendered its representative form of government.

That is the danger for every republic. That was the foundation of the U.S. Nowhere does the U.S. Constitution mention a democracy. Blind patriotism often backfires. Later, to their regret, people may find they've surrendered basic rights during a hot flash of patriotic fervor. It is like a drunken stupor.

In Eckankar, we recognize the imperfection of life on earth, and we do fulfill our duties to the state. However, we're always mindful of our calling to God. It comes first.

Workbook:
Spiritual Freedom

Key Insights
from This Chapter

- Love yourself.

- Love others.

- Love God.

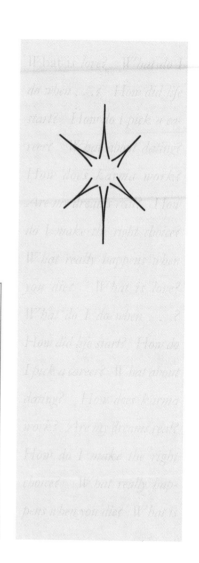

My key insights:

Spiritual Exercises to Explore These Insights

1. Life is about making choices that give us and others more spiritual freedom, in service to all life. Think of a decision you need to make in your life now. In your spiritual exercises ask the Mahanta to help you see which choice will be the best outcome for all.

    Record your insights here:

2. After reading this chapter, what does spiritual freedom mean to you?

    Write your thoughts here:

What does it mean to give spiritual freedom to others? And how can you do it?

Note your ideas here:

3. Create a spiritual exercise that teaches you more about spiritual freedom. It may be as simple as asking to be shown examples of spiritual freedom in your dreams. Or it may be something else. Just ask God to show you, in a way you can understand, about spiritual freedom and what it can mean to you. Then pay attention to what life brings you.

   Record your insights here:

4. Take a moment to go within and realize that as Soul you can
    have spiritual freedom in this lifetime. Look at yourself as Soul.
    As a spiritual being, you are the very best you can be.

    What qualities do you have?

    _____

    _____

    _____

    _____

    How can you express these qualities in your daily life?

    _____

    _____

    _____

    _____

    What additional qualities would you like to develop in yourself?

    _____

    _____

    _____

    _____

5. You are Soul, here to learn spiritual lessons every day. What have you learned about yourself as you read this chapter?

As Soul, a spark of God, you are a light and inspiration to others.

8

CLIMBING THE SPIRITUAL LADDER

Our Reason for Being Here

What is Soul and why are we here?

Opinions about Soul outnumber people's opinions about politics. People who *know*—actually know, not just believe—that Soul outlives death enjoy happy, creative lives. The rest are miserable and afraid.

People who fear hell fall for the trap that Soul can be burned by fire. That's really sad. Soul exists because God loves It. Its destiny is to become a Co-worker with God.

Plato told of the separation of Soul from the body. The old Greek mystery schools taught their students that Soul could reach the altar of God through certain secret methods. The students spent a few minutes a day with unique contemplative exercises that opened them little by little to the Light and Sound of God. That gave them unshakable proof that Soul lives forever.

People who *know*—actually know, not just believe—that Soul outlives death enjoy happy, creative lives.

187

Soul just is.

What being Soul means to me:

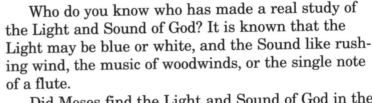

Who do you know who has made a real study of the Light and Sound of God? It is known that the Light may be blue or white, and the Sound like rushing wind, the music of woodwinds, or the single note of a flute.

Did Moses find the Light and Sound of God in the burning bush? Surely the Apostles did experience the Holy Spirit at Pentecost. What about Saul's conversion on the road to Damascus?

Eckankar is a way that somebody such as you or I can bend the odds a little in favor of our having such experiences.

How Were We Created?

Did God create all Souls at the same time? If yes, why? And if not, why not?

In our world, we must think about time. Even your question says "at the same time." But God, also known as Sugmad in the ancient teachings, created Souls before time began, so it is not a question of Souls made sooner or later. As humans, we find this hard to understand.

Yet even when studying the origin of this universe, scientists run into a problem of how to determine the age of the big bang. It's a theory about the moment of creation. But creation happened before there was time. So scientists work from there and accept the fact of creation, because the evidence is all around. However, they cannot fix a date to the beginning of time. It's simply not possible.

Sugmad created all Souls before time began, so there is no answer to your question of when. If God creates more Souls, that also happens beyond the laws of time and space.

Soul just is.

We know that Soul exists by the evidence of life around us. When Soul inhabits a body, that body lives, moves, and has being. When Soul leaves, the body no longer lives, moves, or has being. What has left? By direct and indirect evidence, we know that some unseen force gives life to a physical body.

What is that something? Soul, of course.

There is no simple reply to your question. But, spiritually, there is an answer. In contemplation, ask the Mahanta to let you see and know about the creation and nature of Soul. If you are sincere, he will show you.

The most important point of all is that you are Soul. Know that you are a spark of God and can exist fully only within the realization of that profound truth. As such, you are a light and inspiration to others.

Spiritual Skills

Can Soul operate more than one physical body at a time on this planet?

Yes, it can. But it is a skill usually reserved for those who have put a great deal of energy into spiritual unfoldment, like the ECK Masters.

Some of the old saints could run two or more bodies at once. A case in point is Padre Pio, who gave his whole life in service to God. How many are willing and able to do that?

What Is Our Nature as Soul?

I have many questions about the nature of Soul. For example, do minerals, plants, and animals have Souls?

An uncountable number of Souls exist in creation. There is also an endless number of forms in which

> Know that you are a spark of God and can exist fully only within the realization of that profound truth. As such, you are a light and inspiration to others.

How I am a light and inspiration to others:

Earth allows several levels for Soul to gain experiences in life, including the mineral, plant, fish, animal, and human stages.

What are some of the special lessons Soul can learn in the human stage?

Souls can find expression for spiritual unfoldment. The human form is but one of many.

On earth, we are familiar mainly with human, animal, reptile, fish, plant, and even mineral forms (like rocks, etc.).

We are a little like the theologians and others of the early Middle Ages. They believed that all human races were then known. Of course, the sea explorations by Columbus and others later revealed two whole continents (North and South America) inhabited by a previously unknown red race. That discovery was a major threat to biblical interpretation. Red people? The Bible didn't say anything about a red race.

The Christian Bible says nothing about Souls inhabiting forms other than humans either. Nor does it say anything about Souls living on other planets in forms not quite human. Yet Souls do.

Soul can take many different approaches to reach purification. For example, earth allows several levels for Soul to gain experiences in life, including the mineral, plant, fish, animal, and human stages.

But there's no fixed spiritual law about a rock having to stay a rock. Or a daisy staying a daisy.

By choice, though, most Souls want to taste life at all levels. They do go from the lower to higher body forms. So animals could move up to human. Yet that would take many lifetimes.

Sometimes, in a spirit of fun, we ask, "Why on earth would a cat want to be a kid? It's more fun to be a cat."

(But do you think a cat would go back to being a mouse? Probably not.)

Souls in animal forms do not get the initiations as we do. Their spiritual unfoldment is handled in other ways.

A Soul that today inhabits an animal form will later be offered other life-forms, perhaps even human, when It is ready for a higher stage.

Entering a human body on the physical plane is indeed an optimal experience for all Souls who are given that choice. But the same is also true for Souls who are given the choice to enter an animal or plant form.

The point: Everything is within its rightful place in the Kingdoms of God.

Since Soul is invisible, for the most part, and not subject to analysis in a scientific laboratory, Its nature remains a matter of speculative belief or personal experience.

The purpose of the Eckankar teachings is to give the individual proof of the nature of Soul in a way that is meaningful to him. When and how this is done depends upon the Mahanta, who determines the best time and place.

Levels of Heaven

Where is heaven? What is heaven?

Heaven is inside us. No one can point to a place and say, "It's here," or "It's there." It is a state of consciousness. As Soul moves to higher states of consciousness, It may choose to live and serve in places of more love and beauty. So people think that heaven is a place.

Higher Souls may live in finer places.

Yet heaven is not a place. It is a state of consciousness.

To give you an example, a child born into a family of wealth may enjoy every pleasure and still be unhappy. A sort of hell.

Again, a poor country child may be very happy with so many things to see and do. A heaven on earth.

There are few fixed rules about Soul's path to God as humans understand them. Yet they exist.

Heaven is inside us. No one can point to a place and say, "It's here," or "It's there." It is a state of consciousness.

What heaven is like to me:

> God created Souls so that It could come into an expanding awareness of Itself through their experiences of *love and mercy* toward others.

How I experience love and mercy toward others:

Expanding Awareness

Why did Soul have to come into the lower worlds? Did it do something bad in heaven and have to be punished?

Thank you for your thoughtful question about Soul and Its arrival in the lower worlds. These Souls did nothing so *bad* as to have to be sent here, except that they needed to move to the next phase in God's purpose for creating them. Please understand that the true spiritual worlds above the Fifth (Soul) Plane do not come under the laws of logic from the Mental Plane. You may or may not have trouble understanding this.

Sugmad (God) created Souls so that It could come into an expanding awareness of Itself through their experiences of *love and mercy* toward others. See?

The Souls at play in the spiritual worlds fulfilled a part of God's self-discovery (if we can even use that word). After watching Souls at play for a while (again, time and space have no relevance in the spiritual worlds. They are merely a convenience for us when trying to communicate in human languages—all still from the Mental Plane), Sugmad was ready for a whole new level of an expanding awareness of Itself. Soul exists because God loves It.

This element of God—expanding awareness—also underlies the "plus element" of the ECK teachings. That is, there is always one more heaven. Always one more state of consciousness above the last.

How Did Life Begin?

Can you please tell me how life on earth began? If it came from another planet, how did it begin there? If God created life, how did It do it?

Believe it or not, people of all faiths have asked this question in one form or another ever since the dawn of history. All religions have their own answers.

The Shariyat-Ki-Sugmad, Book One, of the ECK scriptures might sound like tough reading for a young person, but I think you're old enough to handle it. Read two parts.

First, read the first two pages of chapter 1, "The ECK—The Divine Voice of Sugmad." That's to get a sense of how creation began.

Second, read chapter 3, "The Doctrine of the ECK Marg." It gives most of the details about how life began on earth. I hope you follow through on this. It is a fascinating study.

At night, please be sure to watch your dreams. Often they fill in some of the details not recorded in *The Shariyat.*

Be sure to watch your dreams.
Often they fill in some of the details not recorded in *The Shariyat.*

Who Was the First Person?

Who was the first person and how did that person get here?

The first person had no name. Speech, of course, had not developed yet, because names are like labels that people create to call one and not another. So, speech takes people, more than one. Even more than two or three or four, or so.

It took a long time before people dreamed up names.

How did the first person get here?

To get to the answer, we ask, "So how did the first *two* people, or more, come into bodies in the high Mental Plane?" (Everything here comes in twos.) They materialized. It was a bit like on the TV show *Star Trek*, where explorers in spaceships beam down to a planet.

Record a dream you've had recently. Do you remember reading a holy book?

The first people on each plane were created by the Holy Spirit, the ECK, through the arts and sciences of spiritual workers on the plane above.

Ask for insights on how people were first created:

They just seem to appear as if by magic. Yet there are laws of science at work that allow for an orderly transfer of the atoms that make up a human body.

That's to say, people today have a lot to learn about the laws of science. But the knowledge is growing by tiny steps.

The first people on each plane were created by the Holy Spirit, the ECK, through the arts and sciences of spiritual workers on the plane above. So people on the Astral Plane had the responsibility of seeing to the ways and means of transferring Astral Plane people to the Physical Plane.

What means did they use?

Here, I must direct you to *The Shariyat-Ki-Sugmad,* Book One. Read chapter 3, "The Doctrine of the ECK Marg."

This chapter gives the background for mankind's development on earth. It does *not* say the actual way the first couples got here. You can make that connection yourself. People's consciousness, helped by TV and movie space-travel shows, is now ready to see *one* way that the first people came to earth.

Our scientists run all over the globe in a search for the oldest human fossils. They want to know the age of humans. Once they learn that, they hope to tackle the big question: How did the first human come to be?

The answer would shake the main religions to the core.

Way back, there was no earth, no creation. But Sugmad (God) wanted a place to educate Souls, so the ECK (the Word of God) began to create things. It did so by changing the vibrations of Light and Sound in a certain region. That area became the lower worlds.

First was the Light and Sound of God. Then, at a lower step of vibration, came the gases. Eons of time later, liquids and solid matter began to form: the building blocks of lower creation. The Etheric Plane was the first plane to appear, then the Mental Plane. Much later came this Physical Plane.

Galaxies and planets were the first to form on each plane, and then the ECK began to experiment with life-forms. On earth, these included the dinosaurs.

In the meantime, the ECK had evolved higher life-forms, like humans, on the Etheric Plane. They began to seed the planets there by establishing colonies of mind travelers, who could move from place to place without slow, clumsy spacecraft.

Those people pushed back the frontiers of space, even as our astronauts do today. With colonies all throughout the Etheric Plane, the early ECK Masters began to open a new frontier: travel between the Etheric and Mental dimensions. So the seeding of colonies now began on the Mental Plane.

Visitors from space seeded Earth with the first colonies. There was no first man or woman. A spaceship brought a small group of people here to start a colony. Then somewhere down the line came you.

Someday, and not too far off, knowledge of this seeding of the planets will be common knowledge among people of higher spiritual awareness.

Atlantis and Lemuria

Where or in what country did Eckankar begin?

In ancient times, the Living ECK Master gave the ECK teachings to his disciples by word of mouth. Rama was among the first of these Masters. *The Shariyat-Ki-Sugmad* says he came from the forests of northern Germany.

From there, he traveled to Iran (ancient Persia), where he gave the secret teachings to a small band of

In ancient times, the Living ECK Master gave the ECK teachings to his disciples by word of mouth.

Ways I receive the teachings of ECK:

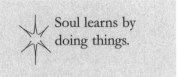

Soul learns by doing things.

Today, as Soul, I learned:

mystics. Their descendants were later to become the followers of Zoroaster, around 600 BC. But the first ECK writings did not appear until much later, around the thirteenth century. Rumi, the Persian poet, was about the first writer to hint at them, which he did in his famous poem "The Reed of God."

After leaving Persia, Rama moved to India, where he settled down. *The Shariyat* says he taught people there about the chance to have the experience of God in that very lifetime.

So where did Eckankar begin?

Even before Rama, the ECK teachings were in Atlantis and Lemuria. Modern scholars scoff at the existence of those two lost continents, so we don't talk much about them in Eckankar today. Yet proof does exist. Under the waters off the southeastern part of the United States are huge stone blocks in the shape of a wall or an ancient road. Somebody put them there a long time ago, when that part of the ocean was above water.

Why Were the Pyramids Constructed?

How and for what purpose were the pyramids constructed?

Your question about the pyramids is a real chance for you to learn Soul Travel.

Soul learns by doing things. Studies show that a person learns faster by doing, rather than by just listening to others. If your question about the pyramids is more than idle curiosity, I'll get you started in your research.

The historical starting point for the pyramids goes back to Atlantis, the continent that once included the Bahamas. It was an advanced civilization that boasted giant pyramids, and they were the inspiration for later replicas in Egypt and Central America.

The Atlanteans had developed science beyond anything known today, including exotic means of space travel for the colonization of nearby planets. The huge continent eventually broke up and sank, but only after many years of cataclysms that left little trace of its former greatness.

During the final series of earthquakes and volcanoes about 12,000 BC, the Atlanteans packed their goods and fled to Europe, Africa, and to the Americas. They took along the culture of their motherland, thus accounting for such a similarity of architecture and customs as is found in widely scattered places like Egypt and Central America, both of which are sites of colossal pyramids.

The Egyptian pyramids and the smaller monuments built in the same complex were mainly for religious reasons. After the death of the pharaoh, the Egyptians took it for granted that the king would continue with the duties and rituals he had enjoyed as ruler in his earthly life. Therefore, the pyramids held a duplicate of all possessions he had owned on earth, for use in the afterlife.

Viewed from above, the shape of a pyramid suggests a flood of light from heaven shining upon the earth. But if one looks at it from the ground level, the pyramid seems more like a stairway to heaven.

The grandest pyramids were from the golden age of the Old Kingdom of Egypt, when the builders still had knowledge of highly advanced Atlantean measuring and cutting methods. This somewhat explains the remarkably close fit of stones in the Great Pyramid. But if we even mentioned antigravity devices as building tools, critics would use that as a blade against the ECK doctrines, which care only about showing Soul the way out of this material prison.

> The ECK doctrines care only about showing Soul the way out of this material prison.

How does the ECK, or Holy Spirit, help you find your way out of this material prison?

Take questions to the Mahanta, the Inner Master. Chant a sacred word, such as the name for God, HU, and ask for answers to come in the best way.

What answers came when you sang HU and asked the Inner Master a question?

Today's archaeologists say that the pyramids were built by slaves, who dragged tons of stone up temporary ramps along the sides of the pyramids. This is certainly true of the later pyramids, which were of a cruder construction than those of the Old Kingdom of about 2500 BC.

In his talks, the Living ECK Master avoids talking about the scientific marvels of Atlantis. He would rather have the ECK chelas go to the inner planes for their own understanding of ancient world history as it really happened.

Here's the way to do that: First, learn all you can about the pyramids from books on Egypt and Atlantis. A strong desire to learn ancient history will tell the Mahanta that you really do want to know about them. Second, take any questions that come up in your research to the Mahanta in contemplation.

To get you started, look for these books in a good library: *Atlantis: The Antediluvian World* by I. Donnelly (New York: Harper, 1949), *The Testimony of the Spade* by Geoffrey Bibby (New York: A. Knopf, 1956), and *The History of Atlantis* by Lewis Spence (Philadelphia: David McKay & Company, 1927).

The reference librarian may be able to help you if the books are not in the library's listings. Or you may visit a book dealer who specializes in finding out-of-print books, since these are old titles.

Saturate yourself with the subject of the pyramids. Take questions to the Mahanta, the Inner Master. Chant a sacred word, such as the name for God, HU, and ask for answers to come in the best way. They may come during Soul Travel, in a dream, or the Master may guide you to a new book.

Research into the past for a study of the pyramids is a wonderful idea because underneath the wealth of history is a pattern of the ancient people who either obeyed or abused the laws of Divine Spirit. Their mistakes can benefit you, if you learn to avoid them.

I hope this gets you going in the right direction. Whether or not you do such in-depth research is entirely up to you. Frankly, if it's done leisurely, a study of this sort can be highly enjoyable.

Greek and Roman Myths

Since there is a grain of truth in all beliefs, what is true about the Greek and Roman myths?

The Greek and Roman myths are legends of space visitors who came to earth in ancient times.

Science now feels that the human race developed in Africa, but few scientists can agree on where the first people came from. What began the rise of civilization? Science doesn't know.

Back in the 1930s, the Dogon people of West Africa jolted many astronomers by the facts they had about Sirius B, a distant star. The star is so faint that photos weren't made of it until 1970. Then how did the Dogon learn so much about a star they could not even see with the naked eye? They insist that space visitors told them long ago.

For now, the people of Earth have their hands full just trying to get along with each other.

Celebrations and Holidays

Why are there no ECK holidays, for example, Christmas, Hanukkah, or Easter? My family celebrates by getting a tree and opening presents on Christmas morning. I wish there was an ECK holiday that was special that we could celebrate with our families.

The people of Earth have their hands full just trying to get along with each other.

Ways I can get along better with my family and friends:

Life is a moveable feast. It depends neither upon a set day nor season, but upon your love for living.

List ways you love your life:

The decorated Christmas tree is a rather recent addition to the Christmas holiday. First introduced in Germany within the last few hundred years, it came a good fifteen hundred years after the birth of Christ. Long before that, the pagan Romans had a fir tree as a symbol for their messiah.

Eckankar already has a day of celebration for the ECK New Year on October 22 and for Founder's Day on September 17. More will appear in our later history.

The holiday of Christmas itself took years to establish. Its celebration was first in January and was more widespread by AD 100. Later, the church fathers settled on December 25 as the date to celebrate Christ's birth.

Japan boasts over two hundred holidays, both religious and civil, every year. It has a long history as a country.

A culture or a society takes many years to develop its celebrations. Be open to holidays and festivals that are a part of your society. I like to celebrate Thanksgiving. Someday ECKists will include it as one of their holidays too. And why not enjoy a Christmas dinner with your family?

The point is that a true holiday is a celebration of God's love for Soul. A holiday, then, is any gathering, even a birthday party, that is our thank-you to Sugmad (God) and ECK (Holy Spirit) for the gift of life.

Make sure the holiday celebration is planned as a happy event. That day, be on your best behavior. It's an ideal day to practice joy, good humor, laughter, and song.

Life is a moveable feast. It depends neither upon a set day nor season, but upon your love for living. That love should reflect your humble love for God.

The Tradition of Santa Claus

I know Santa Claus doesn't come down our chimney on Christmas Eve, but in my mind he does exist. Was he ever real and is he an ECK Master?

The tradition of Santa Claus dates back to fourth-century Turkey. St. Nicholas was a bishop there. Many legends exist about St. Nicholas, the namesake for Santa Claus, but today there is little real information about his life or his deeds.

After the death of St. Nicholas, many people adopted him as a patron saint, especially in Russia. That was long before the rise of Communism there in the early twentieth century. But the Protestant Reformation made reverence for saints less popular throughout the countries of Europe. So St. Nicholas fell out of favor there.

In Holland, though, the people continued to give respect to St. Nicholas, whom they called Sinterklaas.

When the Dutch immigrated to what is now New York in the seventeenth century, they brought the tradition of Sinterklaas with them. He was not connected with Christmas, though.

English settlers in New York liked the idea of Sinterklaas, but they changed his name to Santa Claus. (Say "Sinterklaas" fast and it's hard to tell it apart from "Santa Claus.")

Whether Sinterklaas or Santa Claus, the mission is the same. It is to bring gifts to children.

So the tradition encourages giving.

Whatever name this spirit of giving thrives under, it is certainly a virtue. Both Sinterklaas and Santa Claus are ideal role models. They show that the nature of Soul is to give unselfishly of Itself to others.

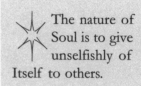

The nature of Soul is to give unselfishly of Itself to others.

Ways I give unselfishly to others:

How it makes me feel:

> The Master's protection reaches into the dream worlds. It touches one's whole life.

Ways I am protected in my life:

Yoga

I've recently started studying yoga, and I love the physical and mental benefits that I receive from practicing it, but I know that many use yoga for spiritual upliftment as well. Is there any conflict with practicing the physical elements of yoga and growing spiritually on the path of ECK?

There is no conflict.

Yoga offers definite benefits in developing both grace and strength through its physical side. Many gain from the spiritual side too. However, the ECK teachings give an ECKist other advantages, like the love and guidance of the Mahanta, the Living ECK Master.

The spiritual benefits of ECK outshine those of other paths. The Master's protection reaches into the dream worlds. It touches one's whole life.

So be of a good mind in regard to yoga, because it offers many building blocks for physical and mental development.

Who Was Christ?

Who or what is Christ? Is it different from the Christ consciousness?

Jesus in fact was the person, and Christ was the consciousness in him. In telling of Christ's mission, John the Baptist said: "As many as received him, to them gave he power to become the sons of God." (John 1:12) Jesus thus came to show people the way to the Christ state within them.

In speaking of "the kingdom of God," Jesus meant the Christ Consciousness. He promised his disciples that some of them would enter it before death. "There be some standing here, which shall not taste of death, till they see the kingdom of God." (Luke 9:27)

Christ was very direct about the location of the spiritual kingdom. To Pilate, he said "My kingdom is not of this world." (John 18:36) To the Pharisees, "The kingdom of God is within you." (Luke 17:21) Yet too many Christians still expect the kingdom—or Christ state—to appear in the sky.

Today, thousands continue to search for the lost key to spiritual consciousness. Many discover it in the Eckankar teachings.

> Divine Spirit has provided many paths for Soul to take back to God. That is why there is no reason to look down on any religious teaching.

The Purpose of Eckankar

Is Eckankar really the direct path back to God?

Divine Spirit has provided many paths for Soul to take back to God. Each path roughly fits the consciousness of a like-minded group.

That is why there is no reason to look down on any religious teaching. The ECK Masters come to enliven, not destroy, religious teachings, because periodically the spiritual light dims.

No one path is true for everyone. That includes Catholicism, Protestant synods, the Oriental beliefs. Many of the different Christian groups are still grappling with the Golden Rule given twenty centuries ago.

A lot of attention is put upon sects today, but the spilling of blood that was the baptism for the rise of Christian power is ignored. The karmic debts incurred by the priestcraft during the past centuries is not where one wants to put his attention. I am not criticizing Christian history, because I played my role helping in the establishment of several paths.

By now you have developed your own ways of testing whether someone's claim has any degree of truth. Use that method and measure the teachings of Eckankar.

Is a path true? What are you looking for in it?

In ECK, you ought to be able to see the Light and hear the Sound of God. No path on earth can promise

What is your path to God like:

its followers prosperity and unblemished health. That is being ignorant of facts, of how things are.

A spiritual path ought to show the way to God. If you find one that does this, then follow it. If not, you must find another that fits you.

Workbook:
Climbing the Spiritual Ladder

Key Insights
from This Chapter

- Soul exists because God Loves It.

- Eckankar teaches how to see the Light and hear the Sound of God.

- We're all on a journey home to God.

My key insights

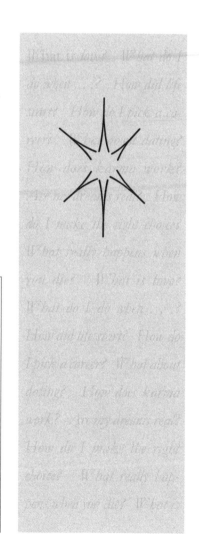

Spiritual Exercises to Explore These Insights

1. Soul exists because God loves It, and Its destiny is to become a Co-worker with God. In contemplation, ask the Mahanta, the Inner Master, to let you see and know more about the true nature of Soul.

   If you are sincere, he will show you.

   Record your insights here:

2. As you climb the spiritual ladder, you become a light and inspiration to others. What are some ways you are conscious of being Soul, a spark of God?

List them here:

3. Each experience in our lives is part of our spiritual evolution as Soul. Think of three experiences in your life that helped make you a better person. How did each one build upon the others?

    Write each experience next to the number below and the spiritual quality learned in the space beneath it.

Write any insights here on how each experience led to the next and how you evolved spiritually:

4. Every experience you have had has brought you to where you are now as Soul. Think of someone who has assisted you with your spiritual growth in this life and write the person a thank-you note here (If you like, you can also write it in a notecard and send it.):

5. You are Soul, here to learn spiritual lessons every day. What have you learned about yourself as you read this chapter?

The Light and
Sound of God
are the most
trusted pillars of
protection one
can ever find.

9

THE LIGHT AND SOUND OF GOD

What Is the Living Shariyat?

What exactly is meant by the phrase "the living Shariyat"?

The Shariyat is the holy book of the Vairagi Adepts. It is a record of spiritual evolution on every plane of God.

The living Shariyat refers to the action of the ECK, the Holy Spirit, as it occurs in creation, before it is recorded in a book. For us, it means the dynamic influence of ECK in our daily lives.

On a second level, the Shariyat is the Sound and Light of ECK. When the spiritual energies of life have been condensed into the written form, we call it a book: *The Shariyat-Ki-Sugmad.* This is the history of ECK in the lower worlds. From the Soul Plane on up, the Mahanta may teach one by direct experience with the Sound and Light. That is also the living Shariyat.

The living Shariyat means the dynamic influence of ECK in our daily lives.

213

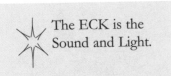

The ECK is the Sound and Light.

Practice visualizing a goal. What happened?

In short, the living Shariyat is every experience in your life that teaches something of God's love for Soul—and Soul's love for It.

The Shariyat is a repository of wisdom that rises from the Sound and Light. The ECK is the Sound and Light.

Visualization Technique

Why can't I see myself when I try to visualize doing things on the inner?

Thought goes before doing, unless you act without thinking. A person who wants a better life than the general population puts his or her thoughts in order by first making a mental image of a certain goal to reach for. To visualize means to see a goal clearly.

If you cannot visualize on the inner, practice your visualization on something in your everyday life. "Practice makes perfect" is an old cliché, but it does work.

For example, if you like tennis, visualize (see) yourself playing a game of tennis after you go to bed at night. Practice your serve. Choose a place in your opponent's court where you want your serve to fall. Practice your serves in your imagination for five or ten minutes or until you fall asleep.

Place your attention on the tennis ball instead of yourself. That draws your attention outward.

If you like some other activity more, like dancing or music, then practice that in your imagination before going to sleep at night. This technique will aid you in recalling your dreams and help you reach your everyday goals. In the end, with daily practice, you will find it easier and more natural to set goals through the art of visualization. You will then discover the secret for creating a happier, more successful life, because you will have a greater say over your dreams and desires. That's far better than letting others run you this way and that.

Do You See a Blue Star?

My mom says the Blue Star is a symbol for the ECK. Is it really a symbol, how do you see it, and what does it mean?

Your mom is right. The Blue Star, or Blue Light, is one way the Mahanta often appears to someone at first. He is one with the ECK. So in the fullest sense the Blue Star, or Blue Light, is the ECK. You'll see it in contemplation.

Of course, the Blue Light *is* real. Looked at like that, it's not a symbol at all—because it is real. A symbol is not the thing itself, just a mental picture made to illustrate it.

To make the difference more clear to you, here's an example: Charles Schultz is a cartoonist. He draws two-dimensional pictures of children, like Charlie Brown, Lucy, and Linus. Let's not forget Snoopy, Charlie Brown's dog.

All these characters are only symbols. They don't even look like real characters.

But we know that the cartoonist's drawings are meant to be seen by his readers as children or dogs, because they somewhat look, talk, or act like them.

A symbol is shorthand for something that is more, something real.

So the symbol of the Blue Light used in the ECK publications is not the ECK (the Holy Spirit) or the Mahanta. It is just a simple reminder of them. A spiritual symbol can inspire someone to become a better, wiser person with more love and compassion for others.

The Blue Star, or Blue Light, is one way the Mahanta often appears to someone.

Find a spiritual symbol that inspires you. Draw or describe it here:

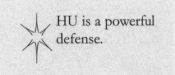

HU is a powerful defense.

Ask the Inner Master to show you what this means:

Protection of HU

Can you explain briefly what the word HU *means and its use as protection?*

HU, a sacred name for God, is popular among members of Eckankar, especially in Africa. Black magic is a very powerful force there, able to wreak havoc. Someone on the path of ECK who is the object of a curse sings this word *HU* and also pictures a shield of white light between himself and the black magician.

The white light is the Light of God. HU is the Sound of God. The Light and Sound are the two most trusted pillars of protection that one can ever find.

People in Europe, Australia, and the Americas also sing HU quietly or aloud to receive protection from trouble or danger on the street, at work, or in the home.

HU is a powerful defense.

How Enlightenment Comes

Can you give me some idea how enlightenment comes into Soul and heals the inner bodies, and what techniques help this?

Enlightenment is a gentle thing if it's right, if you're ready for it. It gives you a different viewpoint, a different state of consciousness.

This also occurs when we do a spiritual fast and keep our thoughts on God, the Mahanta, or something spiritual. You'll notice that when you are on a spiritual fast, you treat people differently at home, at school, or at work. You're in a different state of awareness that day. You're pulled out of the routine or rut that the mind likes.

This actually works off karma. The hold of the material world, the attachments, are not as strong on you. This gives you a little more freedom of choice. It puts you in charge of your own life in subtle ways. Other people can feel this.

Sometimes there is something going on, something that's not too smooth for you. You can do a spiritual fast for a couple of days. You'll find that your attitude and your very words are different. You're not creating karma the way you were before.

Most of our problems are self-made. When things go wrong, if we take responsibility and do something that gives us greater understanding, life becomes easier.

This is how it should be, rather than having someone always giving us spiritual, emotional, or physical healings.

Too Much Sound

I am having some health problems after enjoying a strong body for most of my life. The Sound of God, the divine Sound Current, is very loud. Am I going through a spiritual or physical change?

You mentioned a change of health and the increase of the Sound Current, that aspect of the Holy Spirit one can hear. The natural effect of a changing consciousness can show up as both physical and emotional. It requires us to adjust our habits of eating and perhaps even the spiritual exercises.

In my case, I've found that aging had an effect upon my feelings of well-being. It forced me to develop new dietary habits. I eventually gave up caffeine stimulants, such as are found in coffee, many soft drinks, and even chocolate. The stimulants, on

Most of our problems are self-made. When things go wrong, if we take responsibility and do something that gives us greater understanding, life becomes easier.

What I do to take responsibility to make life easier:

> Everyone and everything in our personal and universal world has an effect upon us. We want to become aware of what these effects are.

Ask God to show you how to nurture the good and discard the bad effects in your life. Write about it here:

top of my increasing spiritual awareness, made me be too sensitive to the Sound of God.

We want the Sound in our lives, but too much of It can render us physically unable to carry on with our daily life. That means we must find a new balance. This means changing our habits.

Go about this rationally. Look at the foods you eat, for instance, then eliminate just the food or drink that seems least useful to you spiritually. Continue to eat and drink your other foods and beverages. Watch for a few days if the removal of a certain food had any beneficial effect upon your feelings of well-being. If it did, don't use that food for several weeks. Later, you may wish to experiment: try to eat it again, but observe the effect it has upon your feelings of well-being.

Follow this plan with a second item of food or drink that seems *least* beneficial for your physical or spiritual good. Go slow. You don't want to make massive changes to your diet. It could be too much of a shock to your body, and that would create unnecessary health conditions.

In effect, you're treating your body as a science lab. What you see there is unique: a reflection of your expanding state of consciousness. While making observations on your food and beverage habits, be sure to get any help you see necessary from experts of nutrition, etc.

We *are* a state of consciousness. Everyone and everything in our personal and universal world has an effect upon us. We want to become aware of what these effects are. Then we can sort through them, nurturing the good ones and discarding the bad.

Being Too Open to the Inner Worlds

My mother complains of an inner sound like people wailing or crying. She is not an ECKist and finds this distressing. Could you please give me a suitable explanation which I can pass on to her?

It's hard to explain some things to people who do not know the geography of the inner worlds, as many on the path of ECK do. She is hearing the cry of distressed Souls caught in a purgatory midway between heaven and earth. This means, between the Physical and Astral Planes.

People who are open to such inner sounds are often quite sympathetic to the suffering of others. They are likely to take in homeless animals and are also soft shoulders for the troubled to cry upon.

But their sympathetic nature actually works against them. They do not understand that people have caused their own troubles. This does not mean we should be cold about the sufferings of others, but it does point out that some people secretly like to injure themselves spiritually so they can complain to others about their problems.

Your mother is hearing the cry of lost Souls. These are generally people who died under stress or unresolved personal circumstances. Let her know that God provides for their deliverance from purgatory (she is likely not to believe in purgatory) when they are ready to stop clinging to the sadness that keeps them here. They are in a temporary state, and angels will take them to heaven soon enough.

Then have her sing the name Jesus, if she is unwilling to use HU.

A final note: Faulty nutrition can also open up some people to psychic phenomena. Have your mother check with your family doctor to see that everything is in order in the health department of her life.

> Faulty nutrition can also open up some people to psychic phenomena.

Ask the Inner Master to help you understand the geography of the inner worlds. Write your insights here:

One who communicates daily with the Word of God, the ECK, can only speak words of joy and reverence.

How I communicate daily with the Word of God:

Seeing Light Bodies

I am twelve years old. I was walking in the hallway of my house when I thought I saw a body of light in front of me. My mind said it was just because I was in a dark hallway, entering a brightly lit room. But the next time I had to go down the hallway, I got scared. Was there really a Light body in my hallway?

There are always Light bodies around us. The Astral Plane, the plane of emotions, is at a level of vibration just above the Physical Plane, but sometimes there are dips or drops in vibration. Then people catch a glimpse of the neighboring plane.

Right now, on the Astral Plane, there is a twelve-year-old girl who also thinks she saw someone in the hallway.

When you walk in your hallway, chant HU, the holy name for God. Then whisper to her, "I didn't mean to frighten you either." Don't worry, I'll be there with you.

The Power of Holy Words

Can spiritually charged words such as HU *be over-used, as were* God *and* abracadabra? *And, is it OK to change the inflection, tone, or meaning of such words in songs, jokes, or conversation?*

God and *abracadabra* lost their meaning when people lost the Living Word. The Sound Current was beyond their reach, and the priests could not lead them to It. Perhaps it was frustration with a dead religion that first led people to take the holy names of God in vain.

One who communicates daily with the Word of God, the ECK, can only speak words of joy and reverence. The Sound and Light are his heartbeat and breath, his golden love. How can he then but love God—and himself? Pure and holy songs spring from a pure and golden heart.

This also answers your second question.

How Did God Come to Be?

Would you please explain to me Sugmad (God) and how It came to be?

That's a rough one. All we can say about the Sugmad is that It exists. There is no way to tag God with a beginning or an end, so we just say It is the Ocean of Love and Mercy.

The tiny human mind can never hope to understand the Author of Creation. But we can love God and others.

Fill yourself with love. Then you will learn everything you ever need to know about God and life.

Ways to Expand Your Consciousness

I feel frustrated because I am having such difficulty with Soul Travel. I am new to Eckankar. Can you help?

The problem, as you state it, is the ability to get out of your body. The methods of ECK work sooner or later for most people. But, of course, owing to the individuality of us all, Soul Travel experiences may be dramatic, routine, or nonexistent.

I do my best to help everyone who is serious about being a channel for the ECK to reach a higher state of consciousness in the way that is best for him. It is a foregone conclusion in ECK that whatever can be imagined can also be accomplished.

Therefore, I am happy to hear that you are keeping up with the spiritual exercises. In doing them, you

> Fill yourself with love. Then you will learn everything you ever need to know about God and life.

Imagine you're a bowl being filled with love. Draw or write about it.

Watch carefully to see what the ECK Masters are doing.

Try the spiritual exercise on this page. What did you experience?

are building up the inner stamina needed to go beyond the physical body, and to remember the result.

Try this exercise, which has worked for some people who regard themselves as too practical in nature for having Soul Travel outings.

Before you go to sleep, imagine seeing yourself as a statue. Visualize the ECK Masters Peddar Zaskq, Rebazar Tarzs, Fubbi Quantz, and Wah Z gathered around the statue with moving equipment. (Descriptions and drawings of these ECK Masters may be found in the ECK book *A Cosmic Sea of Words: The ECKANKAR Lexicon.*) Wah Z and Peddar Zaskq each have a crowbar, while Fubbi Quantz and Rebazar Tarzs are operating a tow truck.

Visualize Peddar and Wah Z prying up the edge of the statue and the hoist from the tow truck being slipped under it. The tow truck groans under the deadweight of the statue, but it lifts it. How high it lifts it doesn't matter.

The Masters now move the statue from one place to another—from the Physical to the Astral to the Causal Plane. Fubbi Quantz then drives the tow truck up a ramp into a Temple of Golden Wisdom where they have a restoration room. In this big, empty room the ECK Masters turn statues back into living spiritual beings.

The ECK Masters are all very happy that they have gotten the statue this far. It's a lateral move but better than no move at all. Fubbi Quantz carefully lowers the statue and sets it down in the center of the room. He brings in a few plants, including large ferns, and places them around the statue to make it pretty.

Now watch carefully to see what the ECK Masters are doing.

Each Master has a little can, which he pries open with a screwdriver. Inside is a very special oil designed to dissolve crust, the crust of ages, the kind of crust that gets on Soul after being hardened by the problems of daily living.

The ECK Masters very carefully put this dissolving oil all over the statue. Remember the statue is you. Shift your viewpoint from watching what is happening, to being the statue itself. Feel the dissolving oil being smeared all over you. After a moment, the crust of the ages begins to crumble, and underneath it is healthy skin.

The ECK Masters stand back and look. "There's somebody in there," they cry jokingly. They watch as Soul breaks free of the human consciousness. When this happens, the ceiling opens up and the sun, or Light of God, touches the real being that was trapped inside the statue of human consciousness.

Repeat this exercise for one month. As you progress in the Light and Sound, the ECK will begin to enliven your spiritual pulse. You will begin to listen, and you will hear the Sound of the spheres, which may sound like the wind in the trees.

As you progress in the Light and Sound, the ECK will begin to enliven your spiritual pulse.

What this means to me now:

Workbook:
The Light and Sound of God

Key Insights
from This Chapter

- Fill yourself with love.

- The Light and Sound of God expand your consciousness.

- Realize your destiny as Soul.

My key insights

Spiritual Exercises to Explore These Insights

1. Close your eyes and listen for the ECK Sound Current. It can be heard within outer sounds, like in the humming of the refrigerator or air conditioner. It can also be heard as an inner sound. Look for an inner light. The Light of God can appear as a twinkle or flash of light, in any color, or in other ways. How do you describe the different ways God speaks to you through Light and Sound? This may be in your physical life, your dreams, or your spiritual exercises. Write your observations here:

    Now create a special spiritual exercise, using one of the ways you perceive the Light or Sound of God. Practice it for one week. Describe what you experienced here:

2. Ask the Mahanta to show you the Shariyat in your dreams.

   Write your experience(s) here:

In the next week, watch for the Light and Sound of God in your life.

Record your observations here:

3. The Blue Star, or Blue Light, is one way the Light of God often appears. Look for it in contemplation. Write or draw the ways it appears to you:

4. One who communicates daily with the Word of God can only speak words of joy and reverence. For one day say only words of joy and reverence.

   What difference does this make in your life?

   Record your insights here:

5. The white light is the Light of God. HU is the Sound of God. The Light and Sound are the two most trusted pillars of protection that one can ever find. When you find yourself in need of extra strength or protection, sing HU inwardly or aloud. Fill yourself with love and bathe in the Light and Sound of God.

   Record your experiences here:

6. You are Soul, here to learn spiritual lessons every day. What have you learned about yourself as you read this chapter?

How can you
forgive yourself?
Just do it. Then
apologize for
your thoughtless
behavior and do
better next time.

10

THE SPIRITUAL LAWS OF ECK

Learning about the Spiritual Laws

How can people become self-reliant and independent when Divine Spirit controls everything?

That's a very good question.

Spirit, however, does not control everything. Sure, It is life itself—to that degree, yes. But providing life is not the same thing as living each individual's life.

Let's look at it like this:

Say, Spirit (the ECK) is like your home. It provides shelter, but whatever you do inside is left pretty much up to you—except for the house rules of your parents. So, too, does the ECK provide you with life. But there are rules, spiritual laws, that are a part of living.

Now here's where the play of free will comes in. You have the choice of following or breaking the rules—all, some, or none of them.

Let's see two possible ways of regarding our life. We may think of it as either a trial or an opportunity.

There are rules, spiritual laws, that are a part of living. You have the choice of following or breaking the rules.

233

> Learn and obey the spiritual laws early. Life is more pleasant then.

A spiritual law I've learned:

Those two ways of looking at life also apply to each and every thing that happens to us. For example, you throw a ball wild and it breaks a window. You learn quickly not to do that again.

That's the bad part.

But if you can learn to be careful in other things and not be careless and break something, your life will turn a corner and be more pleasant in a lot of other ways.

Yet here the play of free will comes in. What happens if you stand in the same spot as before and throw the ball?

Right, there's a good chance you'll learn the no-no's of doing that again.

So learn and obey the spiritual laws early. Life is more pleasant then.

The Law of Karma

I am frequently asked by Christians to pray for others, but I'm not sure what to do. They have these prayer chains that seem to have helped many in need. Can prayer affect karma or God's will in one's life?

Your question is about spiritual adolescence versus maturity. When others ask you to pray for others, it's with the idea that God hears the prayers of many petitioners better than the prayers of one. It's like God is an elected official.

Yes, prayer can affect karma in the short run. But overall, the spiritual law of "payment in the true coin" prevails. Two points to consider: First, the healings are of a temporary nature (since even those whom Jesus once supposedly raised from the dead have long since died). Second, the group uses the healing, if any, as a control factor over the healed ("Out of gratitude, you should become a lifelong supporter of our group"). Where is the spiritual freedom?

Furthermore, these people are trying to rope you into their circle of control as well.

If someone is in need, they must ask for your help. You may also offer it. In any case, an offered prayer must be with the permission of the one in need. Members of a church usually give tacit agreement simply by being members there, because they know that's how that church does things.

Yet Soul's relationship with Divine Spirit is an individual one. We accept the fact of karma and reincarnation. A true Christian cannot. It's not a part of the Christian articles of faith. But all suffering is a repayment of an old karmic debt. The repayment of it brings about a degree of spiritual purification.

All this philosophy still leaves you wondering how to get along with your Christian friends. Arguing for or against a religious belief goes nowhere, because it's a strong emotional issue.

The answer depends upon the situation.

A possible answer: "Don't you think that God knows about the problem?"

In the end, choose your friends. There are many fine Christians who quietly follow their own beliefs without trying to force others to adopt them too. Other people are very pushy. You have to make the final decision about your own friends. Basically, do they grant you as much spiritual freedom as you need?

If not, it's time to find new friends.

Someone may ask for your prayers. In that case, say: "I will turn the matter over to Divine Spirit, because of myself I can do nothing." Then turn it over to the Mahanta, who will deal with it.

Spiritual Laws and Physical Laws

Recently, I started a construction business, but no matter how hard I work, most of my money seems to

You have to make the final decision about your own friends. Basically, do they grant you as much spiritual freedom as you need?

Write a thank-you note to a friend who grants you spiritual freedom.

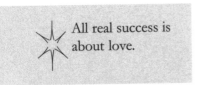

All real success is about love.

What does my happiness depend on?

go for taxes. Are these taxes a violation of spiritual law? What can I do to become a success?

Let's take your concerns one by one. It doesn't take a lot of money to be a greater Co-worker with God. But you already know that. Yet it's in the cards (karma) for some individuals to have wealth and learn to deal with it, in either a spiritual or selfish way.

Taxes are taxes, neither good nor bad.

Of all the people who face the tax problem, each has a somewhat unique situation. Rich people, poor people—some pay too much, while others don't pay at all. You need either to become an expert on the changing tax laws or else find a good tax consultant (CPA or tax attorney) for expert help.

But that's beyond the scope of my advice.

Every country taxes its people to pay the cost of government. Some taxes are fair, while others burden the people, robbing them of the chance for a life of freedom and personal choice. Again, that's a social or political issue beyond the scope of my advice. People who make and enforce tax laws, and all other laws, may violate the spiritual law, but the Lords of Karma will deal with them in good time.

How can you become a success? What is success? It is happiness, and that does not depend upon wealth. There are miserable rich people as well as happy poor people, and vice versa, so don't fall for the illusion that wealth makes for bliss. Nor does it mean a greater ability to serve the Holy Spirit, the ECK.

All real success is about love. Love the breath of air, for it's a gift of life. Love your work: It will expand your God-given powers of creation. And love and serve your dear ones. Above all, do everything in the name of the Mahanta.

A final word: Obey the two laws the writer Richard Maybury gives in *Whatever Happened to Justice?*: "Do all you have agreed to do," and "Do not encroach on other persons or their property."

Success is hard to come by, but love can make it happen.

What Is the Law of Silence?

I often hear those on the path of ECK describe very personal experiences. This makes me wonder, What constitutes the Law of Silence?

The Law of Silence is a spiritual principle that draws a very fine line. If you have an experience that may help another person understand his own, then tell it in a fitting way.

Also be sure that telling your experience will really help that person. Sometimes we like to brag about our imagined superior spiritual development.

You can tell when you've said too much: Your stomach will knot up; you'll feel uncomfortable. It takes some people a long time to learn to watch their own bodies as a sensitivity meter about how their words affect others. But you can learn to do it.

The Law of Silence is easier to learn if you're more willing to just listen to others instead of having to pummel them with your great wisdom.

Someone once said: "Life's too short to make all the mistakes yourself. So learn from those of others."

The way of ECK is one of experience. Use the trial-and-error method to see which inner experiences are too sacred for public discussion.

Keep track of your inner experiences for a given period of time and talk of them to your usual confidants. What happens is that the Mahanta begins to shut down the individual's memory of the secret teachings that are given to him. Within a month or two, you will become aware that the golden hand of

> The way of ECK is one of experience. Use the trial-and-error method to see which inner experiences are too sacred for public discussion.

Experiences I've had where I've learned something about the Law of Silence:

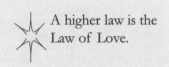

A higher law is the Law of Love.

Ask to be shown the differences between the Law of Karma and the Law of Love. Record your insights here:

the Mahanta's love and protection has been withdrawn. You will feel empty and alone.

When you are convinced of the emptiness that comes of giving the secret teachings of the Mahanta to those who have no right to them, then make it a practice to keep all the inner happenings to yourself. It will take one to two months before the channel to the ECK will open you to the secret teachings again.

This experiment can be done as often as needed. Finally, your self-discipline and spiritual discrimination becomes such that you know which inner experiences can be shared to help others and which are for you alone.

The Law of Love

I have heard the saying "eye for eye, tooth for tooth." What techniques can be used, so our actions are aligned with the ECK? How can we forgive ourselves and not feel guilty when we judge or hurt someone we love?

"Eye for eye, tooth for tooth" is the strict Law of Karma. This law is to teach people self-responsibility. It's unforgiving. Under it, people hope others get punished.

A higher law is the Law of Love. With this law comes the understanding that indeed what will be will be. But the difference here is that we do not wish or expect others to get punished for their misdeeds. Instead, we give them love in return.

How does this work out in daily life?

If someone cheats us out of our property or goods, we will, of course, try to get it back by whatever legal means possible. The difference is that we will do so without feelings of hatred or anger. Such feelings tie us to the strict Law of Karma.

How can you forgive yourself? Just do it. Apologize, then, for your thoughtless behavior and try to do better next time. Don't just try—do it.

And always apologize with thoughts of the Master's love for you.

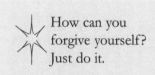

How can you forgive yourself? Just do it.

Subtle Aspects of the Law of Karma

Do plants have Souls? Assuming that they do, do animals get the same karma for killing plants that a person would get for harming another human being?

Just for a minute, shut your eyes and look at life here on earth in a different way. Think of the trees, people, animals, buildings, and every other thing as fields of energy instead of objects you can touch. All these trillion balls of energy weave and blend into one big ball of energy: earth.

Now think of the Law of Karma. What is it? It is only the ECK giving a balance to each ball of energy within its sphere of influence in these lower worlds. Then what is karma for? It is to spiritually uplift each Soul. And the Law of Karma only appears to be more exact for people than for animals or plants because we are looking at karma with a special interest in our own case.

So how karma works depends then upon where each Soul (in human, animal, plant, insect, or even a smaller form) is at the moment spiritually. In general, though, we can say that karma is the same for all. Every act returns to the sender like a letter with postage due.

Do Animals Create Karma?

My daughter saw an animal shelter in our city in which the dogs suffer from very bad care. They live in

Forgive yourself for something. Write or draw how it feels to you.

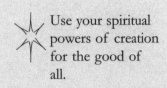

Use your spiritual powers of creation for the good of all.

How I use my spiritual powers of creation:

extremely small boxes made out of concrete blocks. Some of these dogs have gone crazy. Since we both love animals, my daughter wants to know why these dogs have to suffer so badly and live under such cruel conditions.

When people suffer and live in bad circumstances, I can explain it with the Law of Karma and rebirth. But how can those animals have broken the spiritual laws? I didn't know how to answer her question. Could you please explain if animals create karma too, and if so, how?

Suffering is not always a direct result of breaking a spiritual law. Even though everyone gets *adi karma*, the primal karma that starts us off in our first lifetime, there is far more to the spiritual journey. A Soul may intentionally choose a hard life to learn more about love, wisdom, and charity. Pain, like joy, is simply a tool in the toolbox of karma and rebirth.

To grow spiritually, we move beyond a strict acceptance of karma and thus take the high road to God.

You can, as spiritual beings, try to make your city shelter a more livable place. Talk to the owner or manager. If that goes nowhere, visit or call your city hall. Each time, ask the Mahanta what steps to take, then go one step at a time until the conditions in the city's animal shelter are more humane.

An ECKist need not be a helpless cog in the machinery of life. You answer to a higher law: divine love. Use your spiritual powers of creation for the good of all.

The Law of Gratitude

I am fifteen and I like to hunt. What is the karma in doing this? In your book The Wind of Change, *you said you broke your arm because you shot a deer. Does this mean I'll die because I shot a pheasant?*

Life feeds upon life. In the eighth century BC, the Greek poet Hesiod said, "Big fish eat little fish."

Some Native Americans offered a prayer before the hunt, thanking Divine Spirit for the gift of food they hoped to find that day. The prayer showed a respect for life, while still recognizing the need for physical life-forms to feed upon yet other life-forms.

During my deer hunt, I did not have this sense of detachment and thanks.

There was a lot of social pressure in my home community for men to go hunting and prove their manhood. Deer hunting was an annual rite of passage, but I was starting to have a problem with it. My deepest regret later was about going hunting to please others. The karma that followed was due to ignoring my own strong feelings.

You can hunt and fish. Just hold an attitude of gratitude to ECK for Its gifts of food.

Keeping a Balanced Spiritual Outlook

As a sports fan (tennis in particular), when watching two opponents compete, I often find myself siding with one particular person. Somehow, this makes the match more thrilling and worthwhile seeing. When the match or game is over however, whether my favorite player won or not, I accept the result, with no hard feelings.

Do my feelings or opinions when watching a match or game conflict with what is meant to happen? Is it really important for all concerned to keep myself completely neutral when viewing sports?

Polarity is one of the features of life in the worlds below the Soul Plane. Of course you can pick sides in a tennis match, soccer game, or in the political arena.

As an aware spiritual being, however, you should be able to stop taking sides when your participation could take a negative turn. Let's say, for example, you

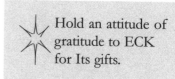

Hold an attitude of gratitude to ECK for Its gifts.

Make a list of all the things you're grateful for:

root for a soccer team. But the crowd's emotions heat up, and the result is a riot. Don't join in.

You do have a balanced spiritual outlook when you can accept a loss by a favorite player without hard feelings. You're on the right track.

Your feelings or opinions have no more or less of an impact upon the outcome of a match or game than do those of someone else. So don't worry about it. Sit back and enjoy the game.

The Law of Discrimination

I have finished school and am beginning to pursue a career. How can I know when to apply the Law of Silence and when to share my goals with others?

Your basic question involves the Law of Silence. But in order to know when to speak and when to remain silent, you must first apply the Law of Discrimination.

So the first question is who do you mean by others?

Be sure of the people you would entrust with the dreams of your heart. Heed the old saying: Never lend more than you can stand to lose.

A sad note about human nature is that the average person will try to discourage a dream that tries to reach beyond the ordinary. I call this attitude the great social leveler. It is afraid of excellence.

So if a goal is very important to you, keep quiet about it—or only share it with one or two close friends. Be sure they have given support to your past dreams and goals. Such encouragement can help.

How the Spiritual Laws Work

Balance is often referred to as an important aspect in life. How does one get in balance—and stay there? Do the spiritual laws help you do this?

Be sure of the people you would entrust with the dreams of your heart.

A goal that is important to me now:

How I use the Law of Silence to help myself attain my goal:

Someone who lives mostly in the outer consciousness is out of balance. This is the social consciousness. Someone who thrives mostly in the inner consciousness is also out of balance, but in the opposite direction. This is the isolated saint.

The balance of outer and inner spirituality is the spiritual goal in Eckankar. Neither too much nor too little at any particular time. That is a determination made by each person. Neither I nor anyone else can dictate what that balance is at the moment.

Every so often someone on the path of ECK says to me, "Please tell me if I ever get out of balance."

Yet when that time comes, he cannot hear my guidance. He may try to follow it, but he is like a robot in his actions. So he continues to make more spiritual blunders. He simply does not understand why everything continues to go wrong even though he is following what he thinks the Master is saying.

The ECK usually takes care of balance by giving certain experiences that restore one's ability to hear spiritually.

How do you get in balance—and stay there?

Always love God—no matter what happens in your outer life. Once you realize the spiritual lesson behind your imbalance, you will return naturally to the mainstream of the Holy Spirit, the Light and Sound of ECK.

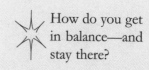

How do you get in balance—and stay there?

List the ways you can stay in balance in your life:

Workbook:
The Spiritual Laws of ECK

Key Insights
from This Chapter

- Live a spiritually balanced life.

- You, as Soul, graduate to a higher level by learning to work with the spiritual laws.

- Always love God and the Holy Spirit.

My key insights

Spiritual Exercises to Explore These Insights

1. Practice focusing on a different spiritual law each day for one week. You can use my book *The Spiritual Laws of Life* or this chapter for ideas. Which spiritual laws do you understand and which do you have questions about?

   Write your insights and/or questions here:

2. Before sleep, choose a spiritual law you'd like to understand better. Then give an invitation to the Inner Master like this: "Please teach me more about this spiritual law in a way I can understand." Then go to sleep as usual. Write or draw any dream you remember here:

3. Grace and respect are two signs of a mature spiritual indi-
    vidual, whatever his religion or beliefs. What are some ways
    you can show grace and respect to other people? What spiritual
    qualities do these actions bring forth in you?

    Make your lists here:

Physical action	Spiritual quality

How do others respond to you when you show them grace and
respect? How does that make you feel? Record your insights
here:

4. A Soul who completes a certain level of purification graduates to a higher level of choice, experience, and service. Take a moment to go within and look at your life from a higher perspective. Your problems are specially designed to purify you.

    Make a list of them and the spiritual law you are learning:

Problem	**Spiritual law**

5. You are Soul, here to learn spiritual lessons every day. What
    have you learned about yourself as you read this chapter?

The key to divine
love is to give
selflessly of
ourselves in
some way.

11

SERVICE TO LIFE

The Secret of Service

What is the secret of service?

In a word, love.

The path to it starts with the Mahanta, the Living ECK Master. The path connects to the ECK Audible Life Current (Holy Spirit) through him. He guides the chela into the heart of God.

Thereupon the chela becomes a Co-worker with God. *The Spiritual Notebook* by Paul Twitchell says, "He will dwell in eternity in peace and happiness."

You see, service to God is a natural outcome for all who do the Spiritual Exercises of ECK every day. They learn to travel in the other worlds. There they find the spiritual benefits of ECK, which are "companionship, life, hope, love, peace, and self-reliance." The last chapter of *The Spiritual Notebook* tells of that.

So service to others is a natural outpouring of one's love for life. I hope this answers your question.

Service to others is a natural outpouring of one's love for life.

> The key to bringing divine love to us is to first give selflessly of ourselves in some way without any thought of reward.

Ways I can give selflessly of myself:

Healing Loneliness through Service

I have been very lonely for many years, and I don't understand how to bring love into my life. Can you help me?

We all experience loneliness at one time or another. But we each differ in the ability to adjust our attitudes to bring light and divine love into our lives.

Some make a great mistake in thinking that the way of ECK, Divine Spirit, is to withdraw from life. This is not so. It enhances our interests and activities, for we gain insights into ourselves through experiencing a wide assortment of activities, thoughts, and feelings.

The key to bringing divine love to us is to first give selflessly of ourselves in some way. It can be a small service for the ECK, although it can be visiting the elderly or helping with some community project. But we must give of ourselves without any thought of reward.

First, do one small thing for the love of God, something small but important to us.

Loneliness is Soul's desire to find God. The Spiritual Exercises of ECK bring the Light and Sound of God.

How ECK Masters Serve

How do ECK Masters give service in Eckankar?

Their service is mostly quiet and unheralded. They work in the background to support the Mahanta, the Living ECK Master with his mission. The reason is that they understand that his mission is their mission. The Master's mission comes straight from the Spirit of Life, the ECK.

So how could they do otherwise?

Path to Mastership

Sometimes the tests in my life get so hard that I wonder if I'll ever make it to Mastership. Did the ECK Masters really have to go through things like this?

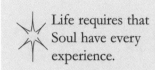 Life requires that Soul have every experience.

Life requires that Soul have every experience. No thought or deed is ever lost—but all is recorded in the Book of Life. Thus Soul learns to have compassion and charity, and to give service to other beings.

The spiritual giants have suffered the edge of the sword that wounded the heart, leaving them to cry in despair to God to give them a reason for their anguish.

The greater our consciousness, the more deeply we feel the slights of neglect, lack of consideration, and abuse by people who use our good nature against us. But there is a turning point where the Wheel of Fire, which is slavery to karmic destiny, loses its power over us. Henceforth we emerge from the fog of unknowing and travel freely in the sparkling lands of ECK.

The Masters in ECK are in a state of vairag, or detachment. It is a state of consciousness that is won the hard way, but when the trials are done and Soul is aware of Its relationship with God, then immense love and compassion are the reward.

You cry with the grieving in their sorrow, laugh with the joyous in heart, sit in silence to listen to the heart of someone who has touched the hem of the Lord. You are an inspiration to the weak, a solace for the broken in spirit. Thus you are a saint, a shining light to all who enter your circle of influence.

Actions Speak Louder than Words

Why don't you go out into the streets and preach the message of Eckankar as they did in days of old?

Each period of history has its own special way to preach the message of ECK.

What I have learned from my hardest experience:

How it helped me grow:

> The Holy Spirit is not bound to any creed or religion. It supersedes them all, for It is the unifying force of life.

What people respect me for:

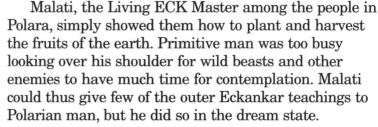

Malati, the Living ECK Master among the people in Polara, simply showed them how to plant and harvest the fruits of the earth. Primitive man was too busy looking over his shoulder for wild beasts and other enemies to have much time for contemplation. Malati could thus give few of the outer Eckankar teachings to Polarian man, but he did so in the dream state.

It would be foolish to talk openly about ECK today in China or in countries where Islam is the state religion.

The public has its many gods and is happy with them. It further believes that the Light and Sound of ECK are merely stories made up by ECKists with fertile imaginations.

Sometimes I play Ping-Pong at a city recreation center. Hardly any of the high-school students there know that I am in Eckankar, but they respect my game. Someday they'll put two and two together, and think to themselves, "Anybody who plays Ping-Pong like that can't be all bad!" In the meantime, I get both exercise and fine company.

This is being a silent channel for the ECK, where actions speak louder than words. And I love it!

Leaders in Other Religions

Can an ECK initiate serve the ECK as a priest, minister, or rabbi of another religion?

The future will continue to see ECKists who fill roles as leaders for other religions. One of Paul Twitchell's chelas was a minister. In Africa, one initiate is chieftain of his people, which requires him to conduct religious services.

Such service to the Mahanta reflects the universality of ECK, for the Holy Spirit is not bound to any creed or religion. Rather, It supersedes them all, for It is the unifying force of life.

Leaders of Tomorrow

Where do you see the youth in the future? How can we help create the highest spiritual community as youth?

The youth are the leaders of tomorrow. Those who practice the Spiritual Exercises of ECK will know how to lead by the example of love instead of the methods of force and lies, which are the standards of leaders under the spell of the negative forces.

These youth will be their own people. Their source of inspiration will come from the Sound and Light of God.

Stars of God (as, indeed, all people are), they will live by the high principles of ECK and be shining examples of a better way to live spiritually.

Such youth will have a community that respects the unique qualities of everyone in it. But even then, each of you will choose close friends from within it who already think and act as you do, because it makes for a happier you.

To help the Mahanta create the best future for all, be yourself. By this I mean, be a reflection of the Light and Sound of God. So keep in touch with the Inner Master. Do your spiritual exercises.

Listen to the Inner Voice of Divine Love

What is the most valuable thing which the youth as a group can offer?

Individuals make up a group. Therefore, all—regardless of age—must check whether they are directed by Divine Spirit or ego.

Do everything in the name of the Mahanta. How? Here come the old standbys: Is it true? Is it necessary?

To help the Mahanta create the best future for all, be yourself: be a reflection of the Light and Sound of God.

Ways I am myself:

Is it kind? Ask yourself those three simple questions every time you are in doubt about any action.

Before a group can be of true service to the Mahanta, each person in that group must know how to listen to the inner voice of divine love. These three questions will help you do that in the best way I know.

How Are We Serving God Now?

If the goal of every Soul is to become a Co-worker with God, what are we now?

You ask a good question. *The Shariyat-Ki-Sugmad*, the ancient scriptures of Eckankar, tells us how a Co-worker with God (Sugmad) differs from a Co-worker with the Mahanta.

Students of Eckankar are Co-workers with the Mahanta. The ECK Masters are Co-workers with God because they have returned to the Ocean of Love and Mercy.

Look in the index of *The Shariyat-Ki-Sugmad*, Books One & Two. The entries under "Co-worker" will give you a better idea about the steps to perfection.

How to Be of Service to Other People

My family decided to invite more people for the holidays than originally planned. I guess I am one of those people who just likes to spend the holidays with family, not twenty-one people.

My question is, should I feel so down when all these people are coming? Or am I being a little selfish?

Sometimes we just feel inadequate. I often did too. We feel as though the success of the party depends solely on us, and twenty-one people is far beyond our limit to serve and entertain by ourselves.

But no one expects that much of a thirteen-year-old girl.

> Is it true? Is it necessary? Is it kind? Ask yourself those three simple questions every time you are in doubt about any action.

> What did you learn when you asked the three questions above?

Next time, ask your parents for a certain role at the party like serving soft drinks, helping young children find toys, or helping guests put away their coats upon arrival.

I used to fear the thought of parties too. But did you notice later how everything had a way of working out, so that you ended up having a good time?

Trust the Mahanta. Sing HU, the love song to God. And try to be of service to other people. Then things work out.

Trust the Mahanta. Sing HU, the love song to God. And try to be of service to other people. Then things work out.

Being of Service to God in Dreams

At a recent Eckankar seminar, I was approached by a woman whom I had never met. She shook my hand and thanked me for healing her of a very serious illness that she had been suffering for some time. This came as a big surprise to me. I was quick to point out that it was not me who did the healing, but the Holy Spirit working through the Mahanta, her inner guide.

Still, my question to you is: Did this really happen? Or could this woman have been mistaken?

How things work out when I trust, sing HU, and am of service to other people:

Yes, this really happened. What you report is a fairly common happening. Other ECK initiates have said the same thing.

As you correctly told her, it was the Holy Spirit, the ECK, through the Mahanta, that did the healing. The Master often comes in the likeness of an initiate to give the healing. He then arranges for an outer meeting later between the initiate and the person who was healed. This is so the initiate can tell the other in plain language something important about the ways of the ECK.

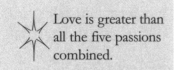

Love is greater than all the five passions combined.

How I am a carrier of God's pure love:

A Carrier of God's Pure Love

What is the difference between the missionary work we do in Eckankar and the missionary work we know from other religions?

A missionary has a message and wants to tell others about it.

But there are religions and there are religions. There are missionaries and there are missionaries. There are messages and there are messages.

In general, though, several forces may drive a missionary, like fear, greed, lust, attachment, and vanity. Did you notice that these are our old friends, the passions of the mind? They tend to show up in the oddest places.

Fear of his Lord's rebuke on Judgment Day may drive a Christian missionary. He believes it's his duty to ensure that family and friends are of his religion and remain so.

Greed may power one's ardor. Let's say someone has started a new church and his salary depends upon gathering a large flock. Also, lust is along the same lines. The missionary delivers his message for selfish reasons, say, he wants to gain influence over an attractive woman.

Attachment plays out a bit like fear. The missionary, for family or group security, wants to convert and keep all within his sphere of influence. Vanity, too, can show up, perhaps, in the head counter. It flatters him to be the missionary who netted the most new converts to his church.

However, love is greater than all the five passions combined. An ECK Vahana (missionary) or a missionary of any other religion who is a carrier of God's *pure* love has no base motives and his message has no strings attached. This messenger loves goodness and charity, and his missionary work shows it.

When People Ask, "What Is Eckankar?"

When people ask, "What is ECKANKAR?" what do I say?

It's best to keep it simple. One answer could be, "It's people trying to learn more about God."

Another possibility is to say that, then ask if the other would like an Eckankar brochure. Here's where you must pay close attention. Some people are satisfied with a simple answer. Their eyes or face will say, "Oh!" They'll have just what they need.

Others want more. This second group will like your offer of an Eckankar book or brochure.

Above all, give those who ask about Eckankar no more than they want. They are who they are, what they are, and where they are—in a spiritual sense. They'd be uncomfortable if they got too much too soon.

A good approach, if they want to know more about Eckankar, is to tell one or two things you like about it. Has it helped you? How?

Listen to promptings from the Mahanta for guidance.

Keep it simple and light.

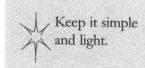

Keep it simple and light.

Ways I keep my service to life simple and light:

How to Explain the Mahanta

How can I simply explain the Mahanta to my non-ECKist peers?

First, try to determine the level of awareness of the listeners. Do they have a most general, offhand sort of curiosity? Then say the Mahanta's like a teacher or a coach. He tries to show how to live a better life—even as a pastor, priest, or rabbi would.

Such an answer often satisfies a general curiosity.

If a questioner persists, throw questions back at him on this order: "What religion do you follow?"

Experience will earn us a place of honor among the Co-workers with God, but only if we master the lessons in all sides of life.

Ways I am a leader:

"How does your pastor (priest or rabbi) try to uplift his church members?"

Listen carefully to the answer. In most cases, you can say, "My spiritual guide does that too."

Leadership

How do youth take a leadership role in the face of views that we're inexperienced, underdeveloped, or naive—without coming across as self-righteous?

Do youth really accept the idea that they are inexperienced, underdeveloped, or naive? That would lead to hopeless stagnation. Yes, it is true that we are all cubs, greenhorns, or rookies while first learning something new. That's life.

Does a high-school basketball coach put a raw freshman on the A-team simply because the new kid thinks he belongs there? Why shouldn't he earn his place on the team, like everyone else?

How does a flutist get to play first flute? She earns it, doesn't she?

All this agrees with the Eckankar teachings. Experience will earn us a place of honor among the ECK Masters who are Co-workers with God, but only if we master the lessons in all sides of life. Some people never seem to learn, and for them it takes longer.

Leadership means a strong sense of responsibility. It is a commitment to seeing a project through to the bitter end, no matter what the odds. Some people are natural leaders and thrive on those challenges, but the rest of us can learn.

To sum up, we must prove our worth, both here on earth and in heaven. That's what makes life so interesting.

Workbook:
Service to Life

Key Insights
from This Chapter

- The secret of service is love.

- Be a reflection of the Light and Sound of God.

- Listen to the inner voice of divine love.

My key insights

Spiritual Exercises to Explore These Insights

1. For the next week in your spiritual exercises or at bedtime, take a moment to thank God for the blessings in your life. With this feeling of gratitude, sing HU, and ask inwardly, "How can I serve all of life?"

    Record your insights here:

2. What does it mean to be yourself and also serve others? What are some of your favorite ways of being yourself and giving service? Write your insights here:

3. Service to God is a natural outcome for all who connect with the Holy Spirit every day. Service to others is an outpouring of one's love for life.

    Imagine some new ways you'd like to be of service to God in your daily life. This can be at home, school, work, church, or in your community. Make your list here:

    From the list you just made, find ways to volunteer in your community, preferably with other youth. Choose one and try it for a day or a weekend. What did you learn about yourself? What benefits did you receive spiritually from giving service to others?

    Record your insights here:

4. For one day meet every person that comes your way with the spirit of divine love and say to yourself, What can I do to make this person's life easier? You may even ask them, "Is there anything I can do for you today?"

Write your experiences here:

5. You are Soul, here to learn spiritual lessons every day. What have you learned about yourself as you read this chapter?

ECK Masters
work in all parts
of the world
today.

Sri Harold Klemp, the Mahanta, the Living ECK Master and ECK Masters
Paul Twitchell, Rebazar Tarzs, Gopal Das, Kata Daki, Towart Managi, and
Fubbi Quantz.

12

WHO ARE THE ECK MASTERS?

What Is the Mahanta?

What is the Mahanta? What's it like being the Living ECK Master?

First, it's a blessing and privilege beyond all understanding. It's a gift from Sugmad (God). God appoints the one who stands as the divine emissary, and so the latter's loyalty is bound by love in eternity.

Second, this position is all about having the doors of learning life's big and little secrets thrown wide open.

Some think the Mahanta, the Living ECK Master has all human and divine knowledge in the palm of his hand. In a spiritual sense, yes.

However, the human mind is but a thimble dipping water from a river. The water collected is as little as what the mind can catch and hold of the full magnitude and glory of spiritual things. Yet a thimbleful of water can capture the quality and nature of the whole river. It's all contained in a single drop.

This position is all about having the doors of learning life's big and little secrets thrown wide open.

> The Master sees the light of Soul in each person. It's the part in mankind that yearns for God.

Ways I see the light of Soul in each person:

Third, the hearts of people are an open book. The Master sees and knows the thinking and feelings behind people's behavior. Yes, he sees the envy, ambition, and greed. But those negative mental traits are in all of the human consciousness, so people's shames are all on the table before him.

Yet the Master sees the light of Soul in each person. It's the part in mankind that yearns for God. That's what he loves.

The Shariyat-Ki-Sugmad, Book One, gives a whole chapter on who and what I see and know. Read chapter 6, "The Living ECK Master." You'll get a look at what it's like on the Master's side of the curtain of life. There are some astounding facts about him, and more chelas (spiritual students) would help themselves in a spiritual way if they read chapter 6 too.

What Is Your Job?

What exactly is the Living ECK Master's real job?

It is simply to help Soul find Its way home to God.

The idea is simple, but carrying it out is something else. What makes it hard is that people forget what they're in ECK for. After a few years, they get too used to the ECK teachings to enjoy living the principles.

It's like a child who knows what the parent is going to say before a word is spoken, because the child has known the parent all his life. Finally, he doesn't hear anything that is said anymore.

The Living ECK Master is to remind the initiate of the spiritual exercises, the three different kinds of fasts, and the monthly initiate reports. Many help him with this mission, and the youths who realize they are channels for the Mahanta are among those.

How Did You Become the Mahanta?

How were you chosen to be the Mahanta?

My training began several lives ago. In this life, I was put into the stern training of strict schooling as a youth to prepare me for my mission in this cycle of time.

A number of people are being tested all the time to become members of the Vairagi Order of ECK Masters, which they must be before they are next in line for the Mahantaship. But first, they have to go through all the Eckankar initiations leading up to that level. The one who is to become the Mahanta is told of his chosen role when he is an adult, but then years of silence may follow as he goes through even stricter training.

All this is necessary for him to overcome the heavy resistance that he will meet from the negative force later in his duties as the spiritual leader. God appoints the Mahanta, and his predecessor announces him to the world.

For me, it was like going to a spiritual school for a long time. There were tests every day. I had to learn to get along better with my problems and with people.

Once I passed those tests, the Sugmad thought it was time to let me have a bigger challenge. It was to help others find their way back to God too.

ECK Mastership

Does the Outer Master have an Inner Master? The chela can talk to the Inner Master, but who do you talk to?

My wife! Seriously, though, when one reaches ECK Mastership, he is responsible to God, the

> There were tests every day. I had to learn to get along better with my problems and with people.

Ways I am learning to get along better:

That's the point of Mastership, having the spiritual strength to lean upon the Unchangeable.

Ways I am growing in my own spiritual confidence:

Sugmad. The Master's direction is always a result of an ongoing communication with the Sugmad.

At first, I found it unsettling not to lean upon an Inner Master, because my spiritual position now had me in that role. But that's the point of Mastership, having the spiritual strength to lean upon the Unchangeable. This means doing what must be done in the name of the Sugmad, confident that no other course of action would answer as well.

It is an exciting position to be in, but it could be terrifying if a Soul did not have Its full spiritual training and were pushed into the role of ECK Master before Its time.

Candidates for ECK Mastership

How is someone chosen to be the new Living ECK Master? And how do you know when it's the right time? Who chooses him, and how can you be sure?

How did a cow and her calf find each other when being separated in a herd in the Old West? Easy. They were of one heart and understood a private means of communication they alone shared.

So is it between the Master and each of you.

It is even more true of chelas who are spiritually ready to prepare for a chance to move closer to, or into, the circle of special Souls in training for ECK Mastership.

The way is long and hard.

A candidate is always chosen by God, the Sugmad. And since the Mahanta, the Living ECK Master and all the ECK Masters, for that matter, have God Consciousness, they know who is in tune with that First Principle.

The choice of each new Living ECK Master originates at the very top of the spiritual hierarchy—the Sugmad.

Unlike a democratic type of government, there is no popular vote. That's a good thing, too, in light of the all-too-human leadership that people choose to represent them. A spiritual Master of the ECK Order of Vairagi Adepts, you understand, is held to a standard far above that of political or ordinary human leaders.

The Christian Bible tells how to recognize righteous people. It says, "By their fruits ye shall know them."

A commitment to walk the talk and keep on the high road to God is a most difficult one. Someone with a great love for God must also have the discipline and *courage* to go in outer and inner places where those of lesser spiritual unfoldment would pale and flee.

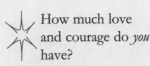

What distinguishes the seeker? Rebazar Tarzs, a Tibetan ECK Master, tells Peddar Zaskq, his chela, it's *purity of character and ideals*. Those are but two signs of a candidate for ECK Mastership.

Would others ascribe them to you?

The only law of the spiritual worlds is pure, divine love. If you want to see the Face of God, know that the experience can blind you or make you great. Do you love God enough to risk the downside?

How much love and courage do *you* have?

If there's enough of both, you will be drawn to God like a bee to a blossom.

And should you like to see the Face of God, what better book to use for your daily contemplations than *Stranger by the River* by Paul Twitchell?

Are You God?

Is the Mahanta God?

You ask a very good question. In light of the fact that the Mahanta, the Living ECK Master is the

How much love and courage do *you* have?

If there's enough of both, you will be drawn to God like a bee to a blossom.

Write about how much love and courage you have:

The Mahanta and the ECK Masters are Co-workers with God.

Co-worker means they work with each other in love and harmony on certain missions because they want to.

Ways I am a coworker in my life now:

How I can improve my skills as a coworker:

Godman, some would say yes. Others, however, are right in saying that God is God and that no Soul in the human flesh, or in any other form, can be the God of All except the Sugmad. And so it is.

In this, the ECK teachings agree with the Old Testament commandment: "Thou shalt have no other gods before me."

The Mahanta, the Living ECK Master is the Godman because he has the highest state of consciousness among all mankind. He is not God. However, he is the ECK, the Spirit, or Voice, of Sugmad. This means that the full force of the Rod of ECK Power and the Mantle of the Mahanta are embodied right in him.

So the ECK, or the Word, appears in the Master. It reveals Itself only to those whom he may choose to accept as ECK initiates. These blessed are the Chosen People.

Do you see?

What Are Co-workers with God?

What does it mean to be a Co-worker with God?

The Mahanta and the ECK Masters are Co-workers with God.

Co-worker means they work with each other in love and harmony on certain missions because they want to.

One Can Become an ECK Master

Is Mastership really an attainable goal?

Yes, one can become an ECK Master in this life. Levels of ECK Mastership exist, and a few in ECK are near the early levels of it now.

Yet many people don't know what ECK Masters do or how they work. Mostly they work behind the scenes, for, unlike most people, they feel no need to prove anything to others about their states of consciousness.

When a Higher Initiate in Eckankar does become a new ECK Master, it is doubtful that anyone around him will ever know. The ECK Masters are humble. They neither seek nor need the praise of others.

The Living ECK Master speaks for the Vairagi Order. So his mission is a public one: to carry the ECK message to the people of the world.

Remembering Better

I do not remember seeing any of the past ECK Masters in the dream state. Sometimes in my dreams, I have traveled with someone, but I never really see his face. Why is this?

The "someone" you travel with in your dreams is an ECK Master, whose name you will learn in time. It is not important now.

Why don't you see the ECK Masters? It is your inner self throwing a ring of protection around your lower-world fears. Fear makes us put off the Spiritual Exercises of ECK. Why? Because we are secretly afraid something out of the ordinary might happen. Maybe the Mahanta would really come in person. What would we say to him? That's fear of unworthiness.

But when the Master does come, the experience is simply different than anything that the mind could mock up. The Master is found to be quite a good friend, and you feel naturally comfortable with him. This is what the person in the grip of fear doesn't know, so the meetings with the Inner Master are delayed until the student is more reasonable in his thinking about what sort of being the Master really is.

The Master is found to be quite a good friend, and you feel naturally comfortable with him.

Ask God to help you with any fears you have about remembering your inner meetings with ECK Masters.

> You can know the Mahanta's presence most directly by a feeling of warmth and love in your heart.

Contemplate on the Inner Master, and feel the warmth and love in your heart. Draw or describe it here:

Here I'll say that you are already meeting nightly with him. It is only a matter of time until you remember. My love is always with you.

Aspects of the Mahanta

I read that the Mahanta can be with all chelas at once. How is this possible?

In his physical body, the Mahanta, the Living ECK Master is like everyone else and can only be in one place at a time.

In the Soul body, however, he is like the air that you breathe. He is everywhere. As the ECK, the Holy Spirit, he can easily be with you and thousands of others in the very same moment.

To put it another way, you can think of the Mahanta as a body and yourself as one tiny cell within his body. Millions of other cells are in it too. The Mahanta is always with all the cells within his body, whether they are in his toe or in his head.

You can know the Mahanta's presence most directly by a feeling of warmth and love in your heart.

Some see the Blue Light. Others find the image of the Mahanta in their Spiritual Eye (the place above and between the eyebrows) or hear the Sound Current.

In whatever way you sense him, he is always with you.

This is one of the miracles of ECK, to be sure. The fact is that behind the face of every ruler of every plane of God is really the Mahanta, the Living ECK Master. The Mahanta is the ECK and is therefore everywhere at once.

This is why every Living ECK Master in history can make the statement, "I am always with you." He speaks with the Voice of the Sugmad, the Word of God, because that fills all space in every plane of creation.

You must learn to trust the Inner Master, but always be aware that the Kal Niranjan can play tricks on you and come in the disguise of the real Master. How do you tell the real one from a fake? Judge him by what he tells you to do.

If the directions you get are those which build harmony and good actions, then listen to the voice of the Master within. Otherwise chant HU and tell the impostor to get out of your world at once!

Personal Dialogues

I assume the personal dialogues in the ECK works were recorded practically word for word. How do the Masters have such precise recall?

Paul Twitchell wasn't an ECK Master yet when he had the experiences recorded in several of the ECK works.

In general, however, the ECK Masters often speak to one with a highly compact form of communication, much like telepathy. It is like a computer program that compresses a document file for storage.

The chela must decompress the file. He tries to keep the intent of the discourse as he converts it into everyday language. There is no word-for-word utility program that will exactly translate an inner conversation into outer words.

It is even harder than trying to keep the exact meaning of a message in English that is translated into French, then from French into Spanish, and finally from Spanish back into English. The several stages of translation can easily jumble the original message by the time it finishes the loop.

What Is a Spiritual Name?

What is your spiritual name and what is the meaning of a spiritual name?

ECK Masters often speak to one with a highly compact form of communication, much like telepathy. It is like a computer program that compresses a document file for storage. The chela must decompress the file.

Try to convert an inner conversation with the Master into words:

Whispering or singing "Wah Z" softly before bedtime may help you meet me in your dreamlands.

When you met Wah Z in your dreamlands, what happened?

Wah Z is my spiritual name. It is the whole name. Sometimes people on the inner planes call me "Z" for short. But it's all my name.

The name of an ECK Master has a spiritual power to it. Whispering or singing "Wah Z" softly before bedtime may help you meet me in your dreamlands. Our meetings there can bring you peace and rest through the night. And some interesting adventures.

Some ECK Masters do have spiritual names that act like first and last names. Take Rebazar Tarzs. Sometimes people call him Rebazar for short. But his spiritual name is Rebazar Tarzs.

Other names are simpler, being only one word, so there's no question about first or last name. Some that come to mind are Milarepa, Agnotti, Castrog, Gakko, Rama, Malati, and more.

Lai Tsi's name has two syllables. Yet he is always addressed as Lai Tsi—no first or last name either.

Did You Grow Up an ECKist?

Do your parents know that you are a top ECK Master?

My father translated (died) a month after Paul Twitchell's translation on September 17, 1971. My dad's job of training me was finished. Many, often including myself, would have found him to be a most difficult and demanding teacher.

In 2001, my mother was in her ninetieth year. She remains a devout Christian and says her prayers before meals and at bedtime.

She is comfortable with Jesus Christ as her Lord. And though she knows in a general way that I have the good fortune to be the leader of Eckankar, she doesn't understand the spiritual importance of that. I write a letter to her every week. The letter is about everyday matters like cooking, her grandchildren and great grandchildren. I try to lift her spirits.

My parents gave my brothers, sister, and me much love despite the often severe conditions on a Midwest dairy farm.

I have much gratitude for their role in my spiritual development.

ECK Masters Have Friends

Do ECK Masters have friends?

They do. The ECK Masters look for pockets of individuals who love God, the ECK, and the Mahanta above all else. They want balanced people who love their families and close ones, and who enjoy the gift of life.

The ECK Masters encourage this small band of truth lovers to carry out a certain mission. Each person in the group is tested often to see how he handles change while serving God. He must embrace the highest ideals of ECK, have a sense of humor, and show good judgment in carrying out his assignments.

The Master in charge does not expect him to know it all, but the individual is to use initiative. He must have the good sense to ask again if he is not clear on a directive.

You will find the ECK Masters to be patient and understanding in nearly every instance. They want you to become an ever-better channel for ECK as much as you do. It is a privilege to be in their company. But often they are in disguise, and their identities are unsuspected until after they leave.

Yes, ECK Masters have other friends too. Three neighborhood cats come by to see how I'm doing. They are the Hunter (a sleek orange-and-white cat), Sunshine (a fat, out-of-condition cat like Garfield), and Nubby (black as the darkest night). They are good company, since they don't have strong opinions about trivial matters.

The ECK Masters look for pockets of individuals who love God, the ECK, and the Mahanta above all else.

What this means to me:

Soul's destiny is to someday become a Co-worker with God. But how many people know that?

What I aspire to:

How I am a Co-worker with God in training:

What Does the Living ECK Master Aspire To?

I aspire to be like the Mahanta. What do you as the Mahanta, the Living ECK Master aspire to?

Yours is a most worthy question.

Of course, you know that Soul's destiny is to someday become a Co-worker with God. But how many people know that?

This divine aspiration in everyone's heart was placed there by the Sugmad (God) Itself. And Sugmad, in a sense, attached a note to this hidden aspiration in the heart. It says, "This aspiration is for me to know and you to find out. Have fun!"

So, for a long time, an individual has no idea what this strange pulling inside him is about.

He mistakes it for a longing to be happy, to find love, to exercise power, to gather lots of worldly goods. But guess what? None of these human aspirations bring him peace for any time at all, even in the long run of many lives.

The Mahanta, the Living ECK Master has but one aspiration. It's the one he came into this life for: to become a Co-worker with God.

What does that mean?

He searches out those people who wish to return to their true spiritual home. It lies in the heart of God Itself, in the Ocean of Love and Mercy. As Co-workers with God in training, they become Co-workers with the Mahanta.

What do they do?

They develop their talents to help the Master search out seekers, whom he will lift in spirit, to one day rise into the kingdom of heaven.

My aspiration? To be a better Co-worker. It's pure joy.

The ECK Is My Heartbeat

Do you shift in and out of the Mahanta Consciousness? And if you do, are you aware of when you are working from there or not?

I am aware of the ECK in, around, and through me always. There is never a moment that I am not aware of Its love and presence.

It envelops my being. I am aware of that every minute and am truly grateful to It for the gift of life. The ECK is my heartbeat. It abides in me, flows through me, giving Its blessings to all, whether or not they accept or believe It. It lets me see the goodness in people, though it often hides far beneath the surface.

ECK is life; It is love. That's why I try to show others their own way to It.

ECK Masters Work in Harmony with the Mahanta

I have a strong affinity with one of the other ECK Masters who has helped me many times on the inner levels. I am thankful for this, but sometimes I get confused about whom I should place my attention on. Should it be the Mahanta, the Living ECK Master or this other ECK Master?

True ECK Masters work in harmony with the Mahanta, the Living ECK Master. The reason is simple, for they are the ECK.

The Mahanta, the Living ECK Master often assigns a certain ECK Master to work with an ECK chela (spiritual student) during a certain phase of the chela's inner unfoldment. The ECK Master is a mentor.

Any number of ECK Masters can appear over the span of one's lifetime to help ease the way. Accept the

> The ECK is my heartbeat. It abides in me, flows through me, giving Its blessings to all, whether or not they accept or believe It. It lets me see the goodness in people, though it often hides far beneath the surface.

How I see the goodness in myself and others:

blessing of each ECK Master's presence. You'll be the better for it.

Peddar Zaskq

Is Paul Twitchell in charge of a Golden Wisdom Temple on the inner planes? If so, which one, and if not, what is he doing?

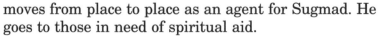

At present, Peddar Zaskq (the spiritual name of Paul Twitchell) is not in charge of a Temple of Golden Wisdom. Like Rebazar Tarzs, he moves from place to place as an agent for Sugmad. He goes to those in need of spiritual aid.

Every so often we touch base. Like all the ECK Masters, the many duties in his care fill the day.

Like my dad, Peddar Zaskq gave me an abundance of both love and discipline. The outer and inner tests and trials were such that I was often at a loss to know where to find the spiritual strength to meet them.

ECK Masters, like Peddar, are like cousins or, better, brothers to me. They and I know and respect each others' missions. We work in full agreement.

ECK Masters among the Native Americans

Was there an ECK Master who lived among the Native Americans of the North American plains? If so, could you please tell me something about him? The Native Americans interest me very much.

Vardrup was the Living ECK Master in the sixteenth century. Originally from Germany, he later sailed to the Americas during Spain's conquest of Mexico. Other Living ECK Masters came to the Americas before and after him, but always in the Soul body.

> Accept the blessing of each ECK Master's presence. You'll be the better for it.

> Ask to meet with an ECK Master; then watch your dreams. What happened?

About 33,000 BC, the Living ECK Master of the time traveled to the Americas in the Soul body. This was Mksha, whose physical area of service was the Indus Valley. At that time, American natives were hunting the giant sloth, the woolly mammoth, and the giant beaver with spears.

One group of Native Americans of 12,000 years ago were the Clovis people. They hunted with spears powered by a hand-launching device called an *atlatl* (say OT-lottle).

Gopal Das, the Living ECK Master who lived in Egypt about 3000 BC, traveled via Soul body to teach chelas in North and South America. They lived throughout what is today Canada, Pennsylvania, Nebraska, Montana, California, Mexico, and on down to South America and Cape Horn.

Among the many tribes to spring from these early inhabitants were the Iroquois, Delaware, Cherokee, Fox, Dakota (or Sioux), Apache, Ute, Comanche, Ojibwa, and the Eskimo. The Living ECK Master of the times instructed them in the ancient truths of Sugmad. He continues to guide all who are ready today.

Simha

I read about Simha in one of the ECK books and decided to look her up in the Eckankar lexicon. This is the definition it gave: "The lady of ECK, who is considered to be the mother of all ECK Masters born in the world of matter." Could you please elaborate on this?

Simha is the nurturing principle in the ECK works. Also an actual ECK Master, she is there to help those in the early stages of training to become ECK Masters.

The Living ECK Master of the times guides all who are ready today.

What this means to me:

She comes to encourage the young. Simha inspires them when times get very hard and the problems of daily life make them doubt their goal of God-Realization. In that, she fulfills the spiritual role of a mother.

Kata Daki

Is Kata Daki the only female ECK Master? Could you please name some others?

She and Simha, the Lady of ECK, are the only two women known in the outer ECK writings.

Most ECK Masters, male and female, choose to live and work behind the scenes. Other Vairagi Adepts of both sexes exist on earth and the higher planes. The ECK works will reveal the names of others later.

Whether man or woman, all ECK Masters cause a deep love for Sugmad to awaken in the seeker. This divine love starts many people on the journey home to God.

Towart Managi

I know that there are ECK Masters who are Caucasian, Chinese, Indian, and Tibetan. I was wondering if there are any black ECK Masters.

There are many ECK Masters of every race. The foremost black ECK Master known in the ECK writings is Towart Managi. He was the Mahanta, the Living ECK Master in Abyssinia, an ancient kingdom in what is now Ethiopia.

> Whether man or woman, all ECK Masters cause a deep love for Sugmad to awaken in the seeker. This divine love starts many people on the journey home to God.

I am awakening to God's love. Describe or draw it here:

Today, he is the ECK Master in charge of the Shariyat-Ki-Sugmad on the Mental Plane.

Men and women of all races belong to the Order of Vairagi. The Sugmad makes no distinctions between age, race, sex, or creed. Neither does the Mahanta, the Living ECK Master. He serves all people with complete love.

> The Mahanta, the Living ECK Master serves all people with complete love.

Continuous Line of Adepts

Eckankar says there has been a continuous line of ECK Masters for six million years on earth. Now we have the 973rd Living ECK Master. This means that each ECK Master would have had to live an average of six thousand years. Can you please tell me where I have gone wrong in my calculations, or how this could be?

The "973" refers to those who were both Mahanta and Living ECK Master. Many Living ECK Masters may serve the interval between each appearance of a Mahanta, the Living ECK Master.

Rebazar Tarzs was a Mahanta, the Living ECK Master. After his spiritual term, he aided those Living ECK Masters who served between himself and Paul Twitchell. If a Living ECK Master translated before his successor was ready, as with Sudar Singh, Rebazar took the Rod of ECK Power in the meantime.

In this connection, *The Shariyat* says that only one Mahanta, the Living ECK Master appears every five to a thousand years. This is a metaphor. It simply means that a new one may come almost immediately or not for a long time.

The image is of the phoenix, a mythical Arabian bird. There was only one of its kind. After five hundred to fifteen hundred years or so, it consumed itself by fire, only to rise again to begin a new cycle.

Use this space for your own journal:

How do you become an ECK Master? Through love and love alone.

Ways I give and receive God's love in my life:

In a similar way, each new Mahanta, the Living ECK Master comes to bring a new level of spiritual awareness.

Want to Meet an ECK Master?

Are there any ECK Masters from West Africa? If so, what are their names? In what period of history did they serve?

ECK Masters work in all parts of the world today. Few stay in a single geographical region for long.

In any age, the chief agent for the Sugmad is the Mahanta, the Living ECK Master. In whatever century and country he lives, he serves every Soul, regardless of race or creed. His only purpose is to help people find spiritual freedom.

Of course, the Mahanta cannot help those who resist truth.

A Master, even from one's own race, is of no help unless the individual is spiritually ready for him. For example, a friend from his boyhood town may find it especially hard to accept him. The mind likes to chew over unimportant details as an excuse to reject him.

If someone fails to move ahead spiritually with the Mahanta, the Living ECK Master, chances are he won't be much better off with an ECK Master from his own country.

Do you still want to meet an ECK Master? It takes a strong desire. If you have it, one will come whether your home is in West Africa, Hong Kong, or South America. He will find you.

Love and Love Alone

How do you become an ECK Master?

Through love and love alone.

However, it is anything but a love without aim or direction. It's all about love for God.

A good primer for mastership that I highly recommend (how could I not?) is *Autobiography of a Modern Prophet* by . . . by—well, his name escapes me. But it's available at a bookstore.

It will help you travel your own path to God.

Remember, love and love alone.

Workbook:
Who Are the ECK Masters?

Key Insights
from This Chapter

- Walk the talk.

- Become a Co-worker with God.

- Remember, love and love alone.

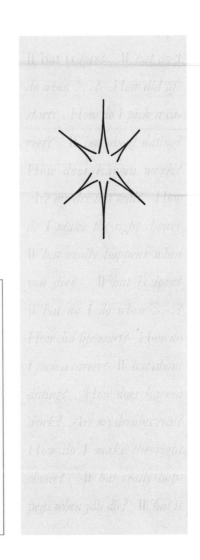

My key insights

Spiritual Exercises to Explore These Insights

1. You can know God's presence personally. In a spiritual exercise this week, feel warmth and love in your heart. Look for a Blue Light or Blue Star. And listen for any sound of God you may hear.

    What did you see? What did you hear? How did this change your day? Record your insights here:

2. The hearts of people are open books. The Mahanta sees the light of Soul in each person, the part that yearns for God.

Imagine your heart is an open book. Draw a picture of it below. How does the light of Soul shine through it? What words or pictures do you find there?

3. One way to meet the Mahanta and other ECK Masters is in the dream state. Before sleep, invite the Mahanta, the Dream Master, to introduce you to one of the ECK Masters in your dreams.

    You can write your invitation here:

    Now relax in knowing that when the timing is right, you will remember your experiences with the ECK Masters.

    If you like, record an experience here:

4. What qualities do you think it takes to become a Co-worker
   with God? Read back through this chapter, and make a list for
   yourself:

Choose your favorite of these qualities. Put loving attention on
this quality for a week, noticing it in others and in yourself.
What did you discover?

5. You are Soul, here to learn spiritual lessons every day. What have you learned about yourself as you read this chapter?

GLOSSARY

Words set in SMALL CAPS are defined elsewhere in this glossary.

BLUE LIGHT. How the MAHANTA often appears in the inner worlds to the CHELA or seeker.

CHELA. *CHEE-lah* A spiritual student. Often refers to a member of ECKANKAR.

ECK. *EHK* The Life Force, the Holy Spirit, or Audible Life Current which sustains all life.

ECKANKAR. *EHK-ahn-kahr* Religion of the Light and Sound of God. Also known as the Ancient Science of SOUL TRAVEL. A truly spiritual religion for the individual in modern times. The teachings provide a framework for anyone to explore their own spiritual experiences. Established by PAUL TWITCHELL, the modern-day founder, in 1965. The word means "Co-worker with God."

ECK MASTER(S). Spiritual Masters who can assist and protect people in their spiritual studies and travels. The ECK Masters are from a long line of God-Realized SOULS who know the responsibility that goes with spiritual freedom.

ECK RITE OF PASSAGE. One of the Four ECK Celebrations of Life. This ceremony is for youth on the threshold of becoming adults, at about age thirteen. It celebrates a personal commitment to the ECK teachings, to accepting the presence of the MAHANTA, and to becoming more aware of one's true spiritual nature.

FUBBI QUANTZ. *FOO-bee KWAHNTS* The guardian of the SHARIYAT-KI-SUGMAD at the Katsupari Monastery in northern Tibet. He was the MAHANTA, the LIVING ECK MASTER during the time of Buddha, about 500 BC.

GOD-REALIZATION. The state of God Consciousness. Complete and conscious awareness of God.

GOPAL DAS. *GOH-pahl DAHS* The guardian of the SHARIYAT-KI-SUGMAD at the Temple of Askleposis on the Astral PLANE. He was the MAHANTA, the LIVING ECK MASTER in Egypt, about 3,000 BC.

HU. *HYOO* The most ancient, secret name for God. The singing of the word *HU* is considered a love song to God. It can be sung aloud or silently to oneself.

INITIATION. Earned by a member of ECKANKAR through spiritual unfoldment and service to God. The initiation is a private ceremony in which the individual is linked to the Sound and Light of God.

KAL NIRANJAN, THE. *KAL nee-RAHN-jahn* The Kal; the negative power, also known as Satan or the devil.

KARMA, LAW OF. The Law of Cause and Effect, action and reaction, justice, retribution, and reward, which applies to the lower or psychic worlds: the Physical, Astral, Causal, Mental, and Etheric Planes.

KATA DAKI. *KAH-tah DAH-kee* A female ECK MASTER, who like all others in the Order of the Vairagi, serves the SUGMAD by helping others find the MAHANTA, the LIVING ECK MASTER. Her pet project is to help people get back on their feet during hardship.

KLEMP, HAROLD. The present MAHANTA, the LIVING ECK MASTER. Sri Harold Klemp became the Mahanta, the Living ECK Master in 1981. His spiritual name is WAH Z.

LAI TSI. *lie TSEE* An ancient Chinese ECK MASTER.

LIVING ECK MASTER. The title of the spiritual leader of ECKANKAR. His duty is to lead SOUL back to God. The Living ECK Master can assist spiritual students physically as the Outer Master, in the dream state as the Dream Master, and in the spiritual worlds as the Inner Master.

MAHANTA. *mah-HAHN-tah* A title to describe the highest state of God Consciousness on earth, often embodied in the LIVING ECK MASTER. He is the Living Word. An expression of the Spirit of God that is always with you.

PEDDAR ZASKQ. *PEH-dahr ZASK* The spiritual name for PAUL TWITCHELL, the modern-day founder of ECKANKAR and the MAHANTA, the LIVING ECK MASTER from 1965 to 1971.

PLANE(S). The levels of existence, such as the Physical, Astral, Causal, Mental, Etheric, and SOUL Planes.

RAMI NURI. *RAH-mee NOO-ree* The guardian of the SHARIYAT-KI-SUGMAD at the House of Moksha in the city of Retz, Venus. He served as the MAHANTA, the LIVING ECK MASTER. The letter *M* appears on his forehead.

REBAZAR TARZS. *REE-bah-zahr TAHRZ* A Tibetan ECK MASTER known as the torch-bearer of ECKANKAR in the lower worlds.

SATSANG. *SAHT-sahng* A class in which students of ECK study a monthly lesson from ECKANKAR.

SELF-REALIZATION. SOUL recognition. The entering of Soul into the Soul PLANE and there beholding Itself as pure Spirit. A state of seeing, knowing, and being.

SHAMUS-I-TABRIZ. *SHAH-muhs-ee-tah-BREEZ* Guardian of the SHARIYAT-KI-SUGMAD on the Causal PLANE. He was the MAHANTA, the LIVING ECK MASTER in Ancient Persia.

SHARIYAT-KI-SUGMAD. *SHAH-ree-aht-kee-SOOG-mahd* The sacred scriptures of ECKANKAR. The scriptures are comprised of about twelve volumes in the spiritual worlds. The first two were transcribed from the inner PLANES by PAUL TWITCHELL, modern-day founder of ECKANKAR.

Soul. The True Self. The inner, most sacred part of each person. Soul exists before birth and lives on after the death of the physical body. As a spark of God, Soul can see, know, and perceive all things. It is the creative center of Its own world.

Soul Travel. The expansion of consciousness. The ability of Soul to transcend the physical body and travel into the spiritual worlds of God. Soul Travel is taught only by the Living ECK Master. It helps people unfold spiritually and can provide proof of the existence of God and life after death.

Sound and Light of ECK. The Holy Spirit. The two aspects through which God appears in the lower worlds. People can experience them by looking and listening within themselves and through Soul Travel.

Spiritual Exercises of ECK. The daily practice of certain techniques to get us in touch with the Light and Sound of God.

Sri. *SREE* A title of spiritual respect, similar to reverend or pastor, used for those who have attained the Kingdom of God. In Eckankar, it is reserved for the Mahanta, the Living ECK Master.

Sugmad. *SOOG-mahd* A sacred name for God. Sugmad is neither masculine nor feminine; It is the source of all life.

Temple(s) of Golden Wisdom. These Golden Wisdom Temples are spiritual temples which exist on the various planes—from the Physical to the Anami Lok; chelas of Eckankar are taken to the temples in the Soul body to be educated in the divine knowledge; the different sections of the Shariyat-Ki-Sugmad, the sacred teachings of ECK, are kept at these temples.

Towart Managi. *TOH-wahrt mah-NAH-gee* The ECK Master in charge of the Shariyat-Ki-Sugmad in the Temple of Golden Wisdom on the Mental Plane. He was the Mahanta, the Living ECK Master in ancient Abyssinia (now Ethiopia).

Twitchell, Paul. An American ECK Master who brought the modern teachings of Eckankar to the world through his writings and lectures.

Vairag. *vie-RAHG* Detachment.

Wah Z. *WAH zee* The spiritual name of Sri Harold Klemp. It means the Secret Doctrine. It is his name in the spiritual worlds.

Yaubl Sacabi. *YEEOW-buhl sah-KAH-bee* Guardian of the Shariyat-Ki-Sugmad in the spiritual city of Agam Des. He was the Mahanta, the Living ECK Master in ancient Greece.

For more explanations of Eckankar terms, see *A Cosmic Sea of Words: The ECKANKAR Lexicon* by Harold Klemp.

For Further Reading and Study

Past Lives, Dreams, and Soul Travel
Harold Klemp

What if you could recall past-life lessons for your benefit today? What if you could learn the secret knowledge of dreams to gain the wisdom of the heart? Or Soul Travel, to master the shift in consciousness needed to find peace and contentment? To ride the waves of God's love and mercy? Let Harold Klemp, leading authority in all three fields, show you how.

A Modern Prophet Answers Your Key Questions about Life
Harold Klemp

A pioneer of today's focus on "everyday spirituality" shows you how to experience and understand God's love in your life—anytime, anyplace. His answers to hundreds of questions help guide you to your own source of wisdom, peace, and deep inner joy.

Autobiography of a Modern Prophet
Harold Klemp

Master your true destiny. Learn how this man's journey to God illuminates the way for you too. Dare to explore the outer limits of the last great frontier, your spiritual worlds! The more you explore them, the sooner you come to discovering your true nature as an infinite, eternal spark of God. This book helps you get there! A good read.

The Tiger's Fang and Talons of Time
Graphic Novels
Paul Twitchell

Venture beyond the realms of time and space with Paul Twitchell, modern-day founder of Eckankar, and his spiritual mentor, Rebazar Tarzs. *The Tiger's Fang* is the chronicle of Paul Twitchell's ultimate Soul Travel journey, which can lead you to the heart of God Itself and your own spiritual awakening. *Talons of Time* is a retro-classic spiritual science-fiction story that reveals some of the best-kept secrets in the universe! Both are superbly illustrated by former DC Comics artist Mar Amongo.

Available at your local bookstore. If unavailable, call (952) 380-2222. Or write: ECKANKAR, Dept. BK53, P.O. Box 27300, Minneapolis, MN 55427 U.S.A.

There May Be an Eckankar Study Group near You

Eckankar offers a variety of local and international activities for the spiritual seeker. With hundreds of study groups worldwide, Eckankar is near you! Many areas have Eckankar centers where you can browse through the books in a quiet, unpressured environment, talk with others who share an interest in this ancient teaching, and attend beginning discussion classes on how to gain the attributes of Soul: wisdom, power, love, and freedom.

Around the world, Eckankar study groups offer special one-day or weekend seminars on the basic teachings of Eckankar. For membership information, visit the Eckankar Web site (www.eckankar.org). For the location of the Eckankar center or study group nearest you, click on "Other Eckankar Web sites" for a listing of those areas with Web sites. You're also welcome to check your phone book under **ECKANKAR**; call **(952) 380-2222, Ext. BK53;** or write **ECKANKAR, Att: Information, BK53, P.O. Box 27300, Minneapolis, MN 55427 U.S.A.**

☐ Please send me information on the nearest Eckankar center or study group in my area.

☐ Please send me more information about membership in Eckankar, which includes a twelve-month spiritual study.

Please type or print clearly

Name _____
first (given)   last (family)

Street _____ Apt. # _____

City _____ State/Prov. _____

Zip/Postal Code _____ Country _____